Public Things

WESTERN SYDNEY
UNIVERSITY

Thinking Out Loud: The Sydney Lectures in Philosophy and Society

These annual lectures aim to be theoretical in nature, but also to engage a general audience on questions about politics and society. The lectures are organized by Western Sydney University, in collaboration with ABC Radio National, the State Library of New South Wales, and Fordham University Press.

BOOK SERIES EDITOR

Dimitris Vardoulakis

LECTURE SERIES EXECUTIVE COMMITTEE

Chair: Dimitris Vardoulakis
Diego Bubbio
Joe Gelonesi
Richard W. Morrison

STATE LIBRARY®
NEW SOUTH WALES

Public Things

Democracy in Disrepair

Bonnie Honig

FORDHAM UNIVERSITY PRESS

NEW YORK 2017

Copyright © 2017 Fordham University Press

Library of Congress Cataloging-in-Publication Data
Names: Honig, Bonnie, author.
Title: Public things : democracy in disrepair / Bonnie Honig.
Description: First edition. | New York : Fordham University Press, 2017. |
    Series: Thinking out loud | Includes bibliographical references and index.
Identifiers: LCCN 2016051377 | ISBN 9780823276400 (hardback) | ISBN
    9780823276417 (paper)
Subjects: LCSH: Democracy—Philosophy. | Political science--Philosophy. |
    Arendt, Hannah, 1906–1975. | Winnicott, D. W. (Donald Woods),
    1896–1971. |
    BISAC: POLITICAL SCIENCE / Political Ideologies / Democracy. | PHILOSOPHY
    / Political.
Classification: LCC JC423 .H7485 2017 | DDC 321.8—dc23
LC record available at https://lccn.loc.gov/2016051377

Printed in the United States of America

19 18 17   5 4 3 2
First edition

for Noah Whinston, with love

CONTENTS

I almost always opt out of the security line in the airport. When I am faced with entering the newer, more radiative machines, metal boxes in which passengers must "assume the position," hands on head, legs spread apart, I refuse to do it. For some reason, this machine and the required posture offend me, and I prefer, though I still detest, the personal search that takes the place of the machine when one opts out. My *first* choice is the other sort of screening machine, the older-style metal detector that is like a doorway you walk through. But those are fewer and fewer these days and harder to access. So I am often forced to opt out. The curious thing about opting out at the airport security line is that—unlike almost every other domain of opting out in the United States today (private schools, private water sourcing, gated communities)—one cannot opt out at airport security without announcing it. One must say aloud the words "I opt out." That performative speech act is required. So, of course, I try to refuse that, too. I approach the line, maneuvering to land in the queue to the old-fashioned doorway-style screening machine that I prefer. But in spite of my efforts, I am often directed to the newer, boxlike one.

When the guard motions me to step forward, toward the scanning machine, I pause, and say:

No, I am not going through that.

The guard says: what do you mean?

I won't go through that machine.

He says: Oh. Are you opting out?

No, I am willing to go through security (I point to the other machine). Just not through this machine.

He says: well, you can't choose. You have to go through this one.

Ok. Well, I won't go through this one.

He says: Ok, so you are opting out?

And we go around again. Same back and forth. I insist, I am *not* opting out. I am willing to go through the one machine but not the other. . . . Until finally, when I refuse again to say the words he wants, we are silent together. For five seconds. Maybe ten.

Then he shouts: "Opt out!" and calls for a female TSA inspector to search me. But he doesn't call that loudly. And invariably no one comes.

I wait a few minutes. We are both pretending someone will come. Then I have to approach him again.

Is someone coming?

He says no one has come because they are busy, and if I opt out, that is the consequence. I will just have to wait.

I explain that I have a plane to catch and that I have a right to opt out and I am not supposed to be penalized for it.

Oops. Inadvertently, I have just said that I have opted out.

Perhaps he noticed. He calls again for a "female assist"—more loudly this time. And someone comes.

This ritual episode is not meaningless. Or not only so. The insistence that I *say* "I opt out" is productive. It obscures the real opt-outs, those who have paid an annual fee, had their irises scanned and their fingerprints taken so that they can be whisked quietly and quickly through security in a separate line from everyone else. These opt-outs, who do not need to speak their name, encounter only the old-fashioned doorway-style metal detectors and never have to assume the position. They do not need to remove their baggies of three-ounce liquids from their suitcases for everyone to see, and they do not need to take off their shoes. They have been prescreened. I confess that I finally joined their ranks, after almost fifteen years of the TSA dance I just described. I also confess that I know full well that I was able, during those fifteen years, to exercise my right to refuse the machinery of security because of my privilege. I was never taken to a private room for questioning, and I never worried I would be detained. I don't fit the profile.

The infrastructure of security is a public thing, one of the few we have left. I will argue in this book that public things are necessary conditions of democratic life. But we live in the moment of the workaround, the opt-out, the secret advantage, the sought-after "edge." We can see how public things become unsustainable when we focus on the increasingly differential operations of the infrastructure of security, in which we are all in it together and yet are funneled differentially into fast lines and slow. Action in concert is the lifeblood of democracy. Divisions like these are its pathogen. And so I will focus in these lectures on public things: on the communities that cultivate public things now, on the things that bring us together in ways that are not optional, on the resilience of both the "public" and the "thingness" of public things, but also on the importance of what James Scott calls "anarchist calisthenics" and on the possibilities that remain to be activated and cared for now.

Thinging Out Loud

- جلي ليكُ بيِعِتَينَـٰمُـٰل

"It is not unfair to say that political philosophy has been the victim of a strong object avoidance tendency," says Bruno Latour, in "From Realpolitik to Ding-politik."[1] But, *contra* Latour, it is actually possible to read most of the canon of political theory from a Latour-type Dingpolitik perspective. The political theorist Hannah Arendt, who could not have made clearer her appreciation of the importance of things to worldly existence and indeed to reality itself, immediately suggests the rewards of such an approach when she says, "human existence . . . would be impossible without things, and things would be a heap of unrelated articles, a non-world, if they were not the conditioners of human existence."[2] Philosopher of language Ludwig Wittgenstein also calls attention to our thing-dependence when he notes that "the procedure of putting a lump of cheese on a balance and fixing the price by the turn of the scale would lose its point if it frequently happened for such lumps to suddenly grow or shrink for no obvious reason."[3] Human systems of value and exchange depend on things being things and not, to borrow again from Wittgenstein, "anything or nothing."

What we may add to Arendt and Wittgenstein is the more Latourian possibility, noted but quickly set aside by Wittgenstein here, that objects may not just stabilize but also derail our world, that they not only condition human experience but also have the power to undermine it. Wittgenstein is right that our systems of exchange depend on lumps of cheese not suddenly changing shape or size. In noting that, he reassures us that this almost never happens. Similarly, our transportation systems depend on bridges not suddenly collapsing. Yet, as I will note shortly, they *do* suddenly collapse from time to time. Here Wittgenstein's proviso that they not do so "for no obvious reason" is important. For when bridges do collapse, we go out of our way to find the reasons; we want to make sure the collapse is *not* "for no obvious reason." We do this to hold people and processes accountable for the disaster. But we also do it because, in finding the reasons, we domesticate what shocks our sensibilities: We reassure ourselves that it was this bridge, not all bridges. We thus preserve the thing as something to be counted upon even in the face of its unreliability. One bridge collapsed. Bridges as such do not collapse. We can go on.

In what follows, I am, as the "Thinking Out Loud" series invites me to do, thinking out loud about things and their contributions to democratic politics. Perhaps I should say that I am *thinging out loud*. The project draws on several sources. It is inspired by D. W. Winnicott's object-relations theory, in which objects have seemingly magic powers of integration and adhesion; influenced by recent work in thing theory and vital materialism in which things are said to have a certain comic or recalcitrant agency; and indebted to Hannah Arendt's account of the work of *homo faber*, whose products have world-stabilizing powers. D. W. Winnicott's "transitional objects," "holding environments," "object permanence," and "good enough" (m)others all circulate through the arguments and readings in the pages that follow. So do Hannah Arendt's ideas about the durability and permanence that "things" bring to the contingency and flux of the human world of action and to the endless repetition that is, for her, characteristic of the natural world. Recent work in vital materialism has made me more attentive than I would otherwise have been to the properties of things in both

Winnicott's theory and in Arendt's and to their magical and malicious powers.

The wager of these lectures is that these two thinkers' unexpectedly convergent ideas about stability, adhesion, attachment, resilience, concern, and care—many of these the gifts of objects (Winnicott) and things (Arendt) to the natural and human worlds—can be usefully extended to think about specifically *political* and *public* things in democratic contexts.[4] The idea is to follow what I take to be Arendt's and Winnicott's leads in order to think about democratic theory in the context of object relations and to ask whether democracy might be constitutively dependent on *public* things.[5]

My focus on public things is occasioned in part by the contemporary impulse to privatize everything (though in the United States and elsewhere, "privatization" is often supported by public state power).[6] Nationalists and communitarians have long known about the power of the collective thing, embracing the symbol, the song, the uniform that help make diverse people into a nation or community. They know what is at stake when those things are privatized (you can wear that or speak that at home, but not in school) or criminalized (that practice is against the law here). They understand the importance of public things to national or community identity. Democracies may seem late to that party, but they aren't. They just offer something else instead: infrastructure. This means sewage treatment plants, power and transportation systems, and the like. These may seem less enchanting than the nationalists' symbols and songs. But nationalists, too, know the power of infrastructure to bind communities together. In Quebec, the history of hydropower, fully nationalized in 1962, is a history of Francization and nation-building in which the publicizing of French Quebecois technical and engineering skills played no small part.[7] That the history of hydropower is not just a history of French empowerment in Quebec but also a history of disempowerment and dispossession of First Peoples will come as no surprise to those familiar with the ongoing conflicts of sovereignty in that settler society. Is this a reason to reject public things? It is surely a reason to politicize them.[8] In this instance as in so many others, one community's public thing is the product of an act of theft and dispossession to another. This is not to equate the two perspectives morally, just to note that two communities see the same public thing in different terms. This fact is not necessarily a critique of public things, as such. It *may* be, though, and I am mindful of that throughout. For this reason, I consider in the Epilogue two alternatives to public things, contrasting the public things model with those of the commons and of shared space.

For orthodox Arendtians, sewage, power, and transportation will not conjure the enticingly inaugural action Arendt is celebrated for theorizing, but rather the mundane domain of Labor that she is keen to exclude from politics. Still, orthodox Arendtians (are there any left, though?) will find in these lectures an argument about public things that won't offend too much, since it is also focused on the more Arendtian elements of citizenship's infrastructure, such as public libraries and public gathering places.

I will not define public things—a definition is not needed to initiate the sort of rumination called for here—but I will refer often to examples. These may not line up perfectly under any single definition but they bear a family resemblance to each other. Some are admittedly quite fraught, as my mention of Quebec hydropower already attests. But many of the examples are fraught in other senses as well. For example, a public thing may not be fully publicly owned but is public insofar as it is subject to public oversight or secured for public use. This is increasingly the case for public universities, which depend more and more on private funding, donors, grants, and ever-rising tuitions.[9] In the pages that follow, public things include universities, local, state, and national parks, prisons, schools, roads and other transportation systems, the military, governments, electricity and power sources, including hydropower, gas, and oil pipelines, and nuclear plants, airwaves, radio and television broadcast networks, libraries, airport security, and more.

In these lectures, I argue that democracy is rooted in common love for, antipathy to, and contestation of public things. Without public things, action in concert is undone and the signs and symbols of democratic life are devitalized. In the United States, the president must wear a flag pin, it seems, but the pin's signifying power is underwritten by a national park system, public cemeteries, public education, and more. Without such public things, democracy is reduced to procedures, polling, and policing, all necessary, perhaps, but certainly not sufficient conditions of democratic life. If we leave to democracy merely the practice of electoral majoritarianism and deliberative proceduralism while divesting democratic states or publics of their ownership of or responsibility for public things, we risk reducing democratic citizenship to repetitive (private) work (what Lauren Berlant calls "crisis ordinary") and exceptional (public) emergencies (what we can call "crisis extraordinary").[10] From a public things perspective, it is notable that one of the first things the Occupy movement did at Zuccotti Park was to establish a communal library. Without public things, we have nothing or not much to deliberate about, constellate around, or agonistically contest. There is nothing to occasion the action in concert that is democracy's definitive trait. What Christopher Breu says about the commons is true for democracy as well: There can be "no common without the commons" or, as he also says, no subjects without objects.[11]

Those who favor privatizing public things often invoke efficiency, citing waste in public bureaucracy and sloth among civil servants whose government jobs are said to insulate them from the supposedly much-needed market incentives that make workers more productive. State bureaucracy, but not corporate bureaucracy, is said to be inefficient. Private service providers, answerable to markets more than to governmental mechanisms of accountability, are also seen as more reliable than government agencies.[12] Empirical researchers and lobbyists can argue about whether we will find greater waste in the public or private sectors. But their findings cannot settle the question looked at here, for there are reasons other than efficiency to embrace public things.[13] Public things are part of the "holding environment" of democratic citizenship; they furnish the world of democratic life. They do not take care of our *needs* only.[14] They also constitute us, complement us, limit us, thwart us, and interpellate us into democratic citizenship. This is true of sewage treatment plants and railroads.

Or it can be. The things we bring, build, use, and maintain collectively affect and constitute us, as is suggested by Elaine Scarry, whose *Thinking in an Emergency* looks at the extra-instrumental impact of everyday emergency preparations in Canada, Switzerland, and Sweden. Emergency planners assign everyone a task and an object and the community has emergency drills. Locals know who is to bring a shovel to the scene and who is to bring rope. Scarry emphasizes the community-constituting impact of the drills, but it is surely also the things they bring—or the fact that they bring things—that does some of the community-constituting work.[15] Back at home, the shovel or rope is a material reminder of readiness to help and of community obligation, fragility, and interdependence.

Similarly, or analogously, when infrastructure *crumbles*, it is not only infrastructure that crumbles but also its constitutive gifts of (de)stabilization, integration, and adhesion. We are forced to face the fact that public things do not only support and subvert us in Arendtian ways—providing fixed points around which collectivities may constellate, generating unexpected and self-surprising action in concert—they also let us down or provoke us. When a bridge in Minneapolis collapsed spectacularly and suddenly in 2007, people were shocked by the loss of life and injury.[16] Many were surely also put out by the impact on their commutes. But people were also, and in a quite different way, deeply disturbed by seeing a taken-for-granted part of the urban landscape simply give way "for no obvious reason." It is no accident, I want to say, that when in the summer of 1993 a community of Mohawk people in Quebec protested a town's plan to appropriate a Native burial ground and sacred trees for a nine-hole golf course, it was a bridge that the Mohawk chose to occupy and blockade in protest, a bridge whose iron had been worked by laborers from their tribe almost a century earlier.[17] In closing the bridge, members of the tribe showed that they understood the instrumental as well as the symbolic importance of infrastructure, its significance as a public thing. The impact of their action was intense. For those who were blocked from using the Mercier Bridge that summer, the issue was not just instrumental (how to get to Montreal); it was also political. It was about French sovereignty in Quebec, First Nations sovereignty in Canada, and more.[18] But it was also about the Mercier Bridge, the different histories it conjures for those in its ambit, the different pasts it supports, and the different futures it promises. It was about this public thing's contribution to, or violation of, the complex and crosscutting "holding environments" of Canadian, Quebec, and Mohawk citizenship or membership.

It seems to me deeply politicizing to take seriously the things being contested in cases like this and to grant to those things some agency in the civic contests that surround them and us. At the very least, public things press us into relations with others. They are sites of attachment and meaning that occasion the inaugurations, conflicts, and contestations that underwrite everyday citizenships and democratic sovereignties. This is what I take to be the contributions of D. W. Winnicott and Hannah Arendt to thinking about public things in the perhaps somewhat idiosyncratic way I want to do in these lectures. Sociologists and urbanists will write about their utility, economists and political scientists will assess their efficiency, but Winnicott and Arendt, each in his or her own way, call attention to the power of things to enchant our world, inhabit us, and press us into object-mediated relations with each other and with a world of things. These two thinkers invite us to attend to how specifically *public* things bind citizens into the complicated affective circuitries of democratic life. Both also note the need for care or concern for the things that we use and by which we are used and which may be our undoing. That is to say, public things act on publics not only expressively but also disturbingly, in ways that bind and *un*bind us, an observation made not only by Winnicott and (in a more limited way) Arendt, but also by Alexis de Tocqueville in *Democracy in America*.

It is noteworthy that when Tocqueville claims in Volume I of *Democracy in America* that the first generations of settlers arrived with good habits of participation acquired in the Old World and further developed in the New, he also associates them with several public things to which they are oriented and on which they lavish the care of citizenship. These include provisions for the poor; road building and maintenance, plus officials to supervise these; records of public deliberation, birth, death, and marriage records, and officials to keep and guard them; and inheritance, property boundaries, property, and education.[19] The first generation locates itself relatively unprecariously in the New World (by New World standards, anyway) when they act in concert to establish villages, towns, practices of self-governance, and public things.

In Volume II, however, something has happened. Time has passed. (Volume I begins by describing life as it was well before Tocqueville's arrival, in fact; the focus is on the "time of the first immigrations.") The public things have diminished or disappeared *and* men cannot attach properly any longer, neither to each other nor to the private things that are left. Is there a connection between these two developments?

Tocqueville was especially shocked by the speed with which Americans built and then abandoned their dwellings: "Americans cleave to the things of this world as if assured that they will never die and yet are in such a rush to snatch any that come within their reach, as if expecting to stop living before they have relished them. They clutch everything but hold nothing fast, and so lose grip as they hurry after some new delight." Seemingly stricken by what we would now pathologize as attention deficit disorder (ADD), Americans are said by Tocqueville almost two hundred years ago to be always questing after things but never finding satisfaction in them.[20] Perhaps we should call it American deficit disorder. In any case, Americans, Tocqueville observes, are ceaselessly "restless." They are also, he worries, prone to mere compliance and inauthenticity. They lack the "liveness" to which Winnicott repeatedly refers as an ideal; something like this liveness is what is at stake in the obsession Tocqueville notes with having things, without, however, being able to "relish" them.

Even something as powerfully orienting as a house fails to do the work of orientation without a context of public things to anchor it. "An American will build a house in which to pass his old age and sell it before the roof is on; he will plant a garden and rent it just as the trees are coming into bearing; he will clear a field and leave others to reap the harvest; he will take up a profession and leave it, settle in one place and soon go off elsewhere with his changing desires . . . ."[21] The American is, in short, promiscuous. Incapable of proper attachment to the things that might give order and meaning to a life, he is always on the move.

It may be that it is as a result of living in a fluid world of object impermanence that the equality that, in Volume I, is said to be the unique marker of American life comes, in Volume II, to be a ghostly disappointment that never quite materializes into something real. Americans as described by Tocqueville in Volume II are a society of Ahab-like creatures, forever on the hunt for the white whale of equality, forever coming up short, left manic and melancholic by their failure to catch hold of the one thing they crave: "they will never get the sort of equality they long for," Tocqueville says. "That is a quality which ever retreats before them without getting quite out of sight, and as it retreats it beckons them on to pursue. Every instant they think they will catch it, and each time it slips through their fingers. They see it close enough to know its charms, but they do not get near enough to enjoy it, and they will be dead before they have fully relished its delights. That is the reason for the *strange melancholy* often haunting inhabitants of democracies in the midst of abundance, and of that disgust with life sometimes gripping them in calm and easy circumstances."[22]

From a family of landed gentry, Tocqueville understood the lure of land as an object of attachment and was bewildered by those not vulnerable to its charms; hence his rather horrified response to his discovery of white rootlessness in America. Whatever the reasons for the attachment failures of white settlers, however, there was no doubt as to the coercive causes of the rootlessness of Native peoples in the United States of the 1830s, and Tocqueville reported, at one point in particular, with deep empathy on their awful destruction. In one of the most moving passages in *Democracy in America*, Tocqueville describes the misery of conquest and dispossession endured by the autochthonous Choctaw, noting with care how the people (perhaps stoic, surely traumatized) endured their hardship silently while their dogs uncannily ventriloquized the tribe's suffering.

> At the end of the year 1831, whilst I was on the left bank of the Mississippi . . . there arrived a numerous band of Choctaws [seeking] an asylum which had been promised them by the American government. It was in the middle of the winter, and the cold was unusually severe; the snow had frozen hard upon the ground, and the river was drifting huge masses of ice. The Indians had their families with them; and they brought in their train the wounded and the sick, with children newly born, and old men upon the verge of death. . . . Never will that solemn spectacle fade from my remembrance. No cry, no sob was heard among the assembled crowd; all were silent. . . . The Indians had all stepped into the bark which was to carry them across, but their dogs remained upon the bank. As soon as these animals perceived that their masters were finally leaving the shore, they set up a dismal howl, and plunging all together into the icy waters of the Mississippi, swam after the boat.[23]

"They set up a dismal howl." Such images of first peoples torn from their land are followed soon after in Volume II by the aforementioned description of whites now incapable of proper attachment to land they have claimed as theirs. When read together, those passages press on us a thought: It is as if—in that moment, and for just a moment, historically speaking—the land regurgitated the whites whose leaders had thought *they* could swallow *it*, once it was emptied of its prior inhabitants. It is as if the object of white desire had an agency of its own.[24] Could it be that what looks to Tocqueville like an inexplicable white nomadism is in fact the land's vengeful rejection of those who dispossessed and destroyed its prior denizens?

The incredible power of things and their (in)capacity or refusal under certain conditions to serve as an object (Winnicott) or thing (Arendt) with adhesive, integrative, and (de)stabilizing powers is one of my main subjects in these lectures. Land is just one example of a recalcitrant or accommodating object, but it is one to which I return. I have already mentioned the Mohawk blockade in Quebec occasioned by yet another planned takeover of Native land. In Lecture One, I am inspired by the Unist'ot'en Camp battle in northern British Columbia to protect tribal lands from invasive pipelines and the other invasions that invariably follow in their wake, and also by the efforts of Mayans in Guatemala to maintain their local food crops and practices, learning from their corn the need to resist industrial agricultural pressures to convert to more "modern," less indigenous, practices and seeds.

In Lecture Two, I read Hannah Arendt's *The Human Condition* together with the work of D. W. Winnicott in order to highlight the neglected role of "things" in her work, and the convergence of these two thinkers on the value of care and concern for the world and for others. The topic of land moves right to the center of things, in Lecture Three, as I offer a reading of Jonathan Lear's *Radical Hope* and Lars von Trier's *Melancholia*, drawing on the theoretical vocabulary and perspectives generated in Lectures One and Two. Von Trier's film imagines the end of the world, and Lear's book examines the end of a world. *Melancholia* may be read as a parable of capitalism or climate change and the human alienation and melancholy they engender. Lear's book brings these possibilities together as it tries to understand the melancholy and resilience of the Crow people who suffered under white conquest, but managed to retain some of their land to this day. Lear builds his book around Plenty Coups, the last great Crow chief, whom Lear admires for his leadership of his people through the end of the world as they knew it. I note that Plenty Coups is perhaps a more complex and even more interesting figure than Lear allows but that in any case Plenty Coups had one great virtue that Lear does not note: Plenty Coups understood the importance of refurnishing the world of the Crow with public things.

Uncannily, both "texts" discussed in this final lecture tell stories of young men who face the end of the world, dream the anxieties of their tribe (in *Melancholia*, the "tribe" is an unpleasant and privileged family of irreparable relations), and then work through those anxieties on behalf of the others. Telling the stories of adolescents forced by contingent events to grow up too fast and face the fragility and destructiveness of things, this text and this film, I argue, offer political parables of democratic maturation in which hope and play are crucial resources of resilience, and community members (elders, an aunt) who lavish care and concern on self-doubting youth provide them with a holding environment. They also, importantly, model elements of the practice of action in concert that are fundamental to democratic living together and demonstrate the democratic need for certain kinds of "holding."[25]

In conclusion, let me say directly what by now is surely apparent: *Public Things* is not *about* infrastructure. If it were, the chapters that follow would focus directly and in detail on James Bay, the Mercier Bridge, or the Statue of Liberty and would proceed historically or empirically. This book is, rather, a political theory argument in favor of embracing publicness in democratic life, for the sake of democratic life, because public things constitute citizens equally as citizens, or ought to, and can be made, sometimes, by way of actions in concert, to deliver on that promise; maybe—when they don't resist our efforts, and even then. . . . That, surely, is part of the necessarily ongoing work of democratic citizenship: to join together to build public things, maintain them, and (re)secure them as the truly *public* things—the transitional objects—of democratic life, while also learning to accept the sense of futility they sometime visit upon us when they remind us that they are more permanent than we, or less so, often unjust in their histories and violent in their self-maintenance, and that, in any case, we are not always in charge.

The first lecture makes the case for public things as an important entry point into democratic theory. The second develops that claim further by way of readings of Arendt and Winnicott that highlight their dovetailing accounts of things, while also noting the further convergence of these thinkers on care and concern for the things of this world. The third finds in a dialogue of sorts between Lear and von Trier an argument in favor of play and hope as key elements in a repertoire of resilience that must be part of democratic theory now. The epilogue contrasts the public things model with that of two others, the commons or undercommons, and shared space, and makes the case that while all three respond to the democratic need, public things have their own specific and necessary contribution to make.

/

Democracy's Necessary Conditions

The importance of public things to democratic life is not currently a central concern in political theory. The *res* of *res publica* is unmentioned by civic republicans today, and the attention of a great deal of political theory has been focused for a while now on a host of other necessary conditions of democratic life: just procedures, free and fair elections, mechanisms of deliberation, the constitution of the demos, the security of territorial boundaries, the ethics of immigration, legitimation crises, or the need to rethink democracy in transnational terms.[1] Most recently, Wendy Brown has called attention to the stealthy work of neoliberal rationality, which infects but does not *obviously* overturn such commitments to democratic norms, process, and procedure.[2] The shell of democracy remains, for the moment, says Brown, but inside the shell everything done in the everyday life of democratic citizens and subjects undermines democracy or "hollows" it out further.[3] People are now trained to think of themselves as a resource to be invested in for future profits or earnings, not as subjects of integrity or, as Brown argues and as I, too, would say, stewards of shared futures. Citizenship itself is undone by neoliberalism's unremitting calculations of instrumental worth and its incapacity to imagine a world-building project that is not entrepreneurial by nature.

Proceduralism and process are no defense against this. They are sadly compatible with it,[4] or at least not incompatible with it, and so they yield easily to "benchmarks" and "best practices," which may seem like mere verbiage but in fact promote an epistemic sea change that, Brown claims, leaves the fundaments of democratic life behind.

Thirty years ago, when Reaganism was rife, Michael Walzer, too, noticed the tendency of certain kinds of calculation to bleed into other domains of life to which they were ill suited. His response, in *Spheres of Justice*, was to propose that we think of justice in terms of spheres. In different spheres of life, justice consists in the application of different standards. Thus, justice requires that certain values, like efficiency, stay in their own sphere. Efficiency need not be a vice or a threat. It has its place. The problem comes when we mistakenly appeal to efficiency in other domains, where it is ill-suited, may be a source of corruption and is certainly not just. The conceptual boundaries that distinguish the different spheres should be strengthened, and the boundaries respected in practice, Walzer argued in the 1980s at the birth of what we now call neoliberalism, one of whose chief traits is arguably its imperviousness to such boundaries, and others, whether conceptual, territorial, or national. In 2015, Brown argues that the genie is well out of the bottle. Efficiency is no longer one value among others. It has become rationality itself, and it is the standard by which everything is assessed. It has infiltrated everything; it has no rivals. All spheres submit to its homogenizing powers.[5]

A similar argument was made by Hannah Arendt thirty years earlier still, in her 1958 text, *The Human Condition*, on which I focus in some detail in Lecture Two. Arendt highlights the invasion of the properly political sphere of Action by the temporalities and mentalities of two other registers of the *vitae activa*: Labor (which is all about reproduction and consumption, she says) and Work (which is all about production and product). Once Action is corrupted by these other modes of life, it loses its redemptive and powerful qualities. Arendt sees the rise of bureaucracy, mass society, and consumerism (not yet neoliberalism) as having precisely this impact. Her book charts the decline of "the political" while retracing the lines of its proper circumscription. There is something tragic and belated about the book's story: The horse has gone out of the barn, and there is no getting it back, it seems. Nonetheless, Arendt, like Walzer, writes in the hope that there may yet be a way. Some clarity in understanding and precision in analysis may yet inform our understandings and lead to change. Brown's tone in her book is a bit more tragic still. The strongest notes are those of loss, not mobilization. In Walzer, too, there is a certain "resignation." He acknowledges the fact that many of the spheres he delineates are subtended by traits he himself identifies as corruptions of the proper. This is a sad fact of practice that somehow does not have the power to undo the theory—but does, it seems to me, lessen the power of the theory.[6]

In the context of the work mentioned here by Arendt, Walzer, and Brown, in the context of sixty-plus years of charting the almost always already overness of democracy's (or of politics') necessary conditions, it may seem belated and downright nostalgic (or, worse yet, self-delusional!) to suggest we think now about public things and their role in democratic political life. Or perhaps it is useful to think about public things now precisely because it is not quite too late to defend those we still have, to render them more fully accessible and egalitarian, and to generate or promote new ones if we can appreciate their constitutive necessity to democratic life and act in concert to secure them. Even political theorists currently focused on subjectivation may find promise in such "objectivation" because democracy, whatever its many other constitutive conditions, always involves inaugurating, maintaining, and contesting shared or public things, and responding to them when they call to us, as well.

New York's Central Park was built in an awful swamp, but on it were lavished incredible skills, craftsmanship, design, and materials. This and, in particular, the use of Alhambra style tiles whose colors do not stop at the surface but run all the way through, stands as a great metaphor for public things whose powers run all the way through us. And this lavish care was no accident. As Joshua Cohen explains: "Olmsted had spent the 1850s working as a journalist, writing about slavery and aristocracy. He thought that the conflict between North and South in the United States was part of a global fight between democratic and aristocratic models of society. There's an aristocratic criticism of democracy that goes all the way back to Plato, that when you try to do things for everyone you end up with lowest common denominator crap. Olmsted saw building Central Park as a way of proving the aristocrats wrong. It was built by a democratic society for a democratic society—for the people—and was incredibly beautiful. His bet was that people would be drawn to it."[7] And they have been. At their best, public things gather people together, materially and symbolically, and in relation to them diverse peoples may come to see and experience themselves—even if just momentarily—as a common in relation to a commons, a collected if not a collective, to redeploy Michael Oakeshott's distinction.[8]

My speculation about the power of public things is invited by the work of D. W. Winnicott, who is one of its inspirations. Rousseau—who understood the importance of joy and sharedness to the adhesiveness of national identity—is another: "It must be fun to be a Pole!" he says in his *Government of Poland*, as he lists the things—costume, ritual, food, dance, and so on—all specifically Polish things that may impart a unifying sense of "Polishness" to a people at risk of foreign occupation and the consequent loss of national selfhood. If I turn in these lectures to Winnicott rather than Rousseau it is because, for Rousseau, public things are like accessories to the human while, for Winnicott, things—transitional objects—are key to what makes us human. Rousseau surrounds the human with things that bestow identity. Winnicott, by contrast, sees humans as constituted in their liveness by relations to things as such.

Winnicott makes the case in object-relations psychology for the centrality of objects to the developing infant's capacity to relate to the world as an external reality. The baby, on Winnicott's account, needs its transitional object (the blanket, a toy) to supply it with a kind of object-ivity, or realness. The baby learns about the existence of an external world when it destroys/disavows the object and the object survives. This is object permanence. The fantasy of infantile omnipotence gives way, in the face of the object's permanence, to the reality of subjectivity, finitude, survival.[9] The object thus *thwarts* the infant with its object-ivity, but that very same trait also *underwrites* the infant's own developing subjectivity. The object's capacity to thwart is the same as its capacity to support: Both are related to its permanence. The object's survival of the baby's destruction is how the baby learns it is safe and permissible to experience and express feelings of aggression, rage, even hatred. (In the amazing comic strip *Calvin and Hobbes*, Calvin frequently throws his beloved toy tiger, Hobbes, off clifftops or treetops, and the tiger always survives.[10])

The object's unitariness is also a resource for the developing infant who comes by way of object relations and object use to understand itself as a unit as well. For Winnicott, dispersion or fragmentation is always a psychological possibility and the therapeutic aim is to be (self-)collected, to collect oneself. "Pull yourself together," we say to distraught people who are—we say—"coming apart at the seams" or "going to pieces."[11] The baby has, in intrasubjective terms, to learn to act in concert. She learns about cohesion and unitariness from the object world, and ultimately she takes it on. Now, what if the same is true—analogously—for democratic citizens? That is, what if democratic forms of life depend partly upon objects to help collect diverse citizens into self-governing publics divested (like Winnicott's maturing infants) of fantasies of omnipotence and invested with a sense of integrated subjectivity, responsibility, agency, and concern?

In political theory, where collectivity is the point of departure, we can see how collectivity, just like personality in Winnicott, postulates successful acts of collection and re-collection and that such self-collection occurs in relation to objects. Hence Winnicott's initial term: object *relations*. In political theory, we might attend in particular to the power of *public* things to stimulate the object relations of democratic collectivity. As I noted in the introduction, those public things are the infrastructure of democratic life, and they underwrite the signs and symbols of democratic unity that, for the moment, still survive. The ubiquitous flag pins that even the American president must wear are underwritten by the public things of democracy: schools, prisons, water treatment plants, wars, transportation, and more.

In *Undoing the Demos*, Wendy Brown comes close to commenting on this. She notes the undoing of the demos by way of privatization and by new habits of rational calculation that, she says, have taken the place of public things and civic mindedness. But her primary focus, notwithstanding her discussion of the demise of the public university, is on the educational goods the public university has the power to deliver and on the demos that needs to be educated, and not on the powers of the public thing as such. She charts the loss of the idea of a people united in deliberation and action to build a collective, democratic present and future. She faults neoliberalization, as a result of which markets are everywhere, market rationality governs everything, and the basic terms of democratic life have been lost. Looking for ways out of the problem, Brown is drawn to Rousseau's paradox of politics in which, he says, a good people and good law or institutions presuppose and require each other.[12] In the period of founding, good law is required to found a people but good people are needed to found good law. How to break out of the impasse of the paradox? In the *Social Contract*, Rousseau imagines a miraculous lawgiver who appears on the scene for long enough to get the social contract going by convening the people, setting the agenda, and giving good law. I will suggest here that the lawgiver's role may be played by public things.

I have argued elsewhere that Rousseau's problem of beginning is not a one-time thing but a quandary that besets every democracy every day, as new members immigrate and are born into it, and established members are every day reimpressed (or not) into its norms anew, with varying degrees of success.[13] If, on Rousseau's account, we need a miracle (Rousseau's lawgiver) to get started, then we need one every day, on mine.[14] For Brown, though, we are further and further removed from such miracles now. Rousseau's paradox reasserts itself ever more powerfully under neoliberalism because of the evisceration of the public university system whose mission of civic education is undone not only by underfunding, which requires ever more fundraising from private sources (which drives the university's research and priorities according to values that may be dear to the donor but are often alien to the institution and far from any true democratic needs), but also by neoliberalism's cultivated hostility to anything that is not clearly instrumental, profitable, and practical from the perspective of late capitalism. Without the public university's commitments to liberal arts education, we are thrust back into the insoluble paradox, albeit now with no miracle in sight. Says Brown: "Hence, another variation on Rousseau's paradox: to preserve the kind of education that nourishes democratic culture and enables democratic rule, we require the knowledge that only a liberal arts education can provide. Thus democracy hollowed out by neoliberal rationality cannot be counted on to renew liberal arts education for a democratic citizenry."[15] Without the vision and aspirations nurtured by such education, we are, Brown laments, limited to mere "reform and resistance,"[16] both of which, she thinks, do little or nothing to remediate the bleak conditions under which democracy labors fitfully to survive today, a labor that, Brown intimates, has already been rendered nugatory.

Brown's analysis of the wholesale conquest of democratic life by neoliberal reason and, more importantly, of *homo politicus* by *homo oeconomicus*, is compelling and stark. This particular statement of it contains one of her explicit references to public things as such: "when there is only *homo oeconomicus*, and when the domain of the political itself is rendered in economic terms, the foundation vanishes for citizenship concerned with public things and the common good. Here, the problem is not just that public goods are defunded and common ends are devalued by neoliberal reason although this is so, but that citizenship itself loses its *political* valence and venue [sphereism again; italics in the original]. Valence: *homo oeconomicus* approaches everything as a market and knows only market conduct; it cannot think public purposes or common problems in a distinctly political way. Venue: Political life, and the state in particular, . . . are remade by neoliberal rationality [and] . . . the very idea of a people, a demos asserting its collective political sovereignty [is eliminated]."[17]

Is Brown's case so compelling because it is so obviously true? Perhaps better, we can say that her powerful writing makes what is true about it into something that suddenly seems inescapably obvious. We have seen public universities trade in faculty governance and accountability for private donors, market incentives, and industry benchmarks. We have seen those who once appreciated an institution's uniqueness turn, instead, to talk about its "branding." We have witnessed the craze for "massive open online courses" (MOOCs) as the next big thing, and the sight of universities as unabashed chasers of the next big thing, and we have heard the silence that followed the apparent collapse or normalization of the craze that was originally touted as foretelling the transformation of education into service delivery. Thus, when Toni Morrison charts the transition in her political lifetime from U.S. subjects being addressed as "citizens" to being addressed as "taxpayers," most of her readers will experience the jolt of recognition that underwrites Brown's theoretical arguments.[18]

But the power of the case may also be its limitation. The overtaking of the contemporary mind by neoliberal rationality is so powerful in Brown's account that it is difficult to understand where resistance could come from and how a politics of alternative movements could take hold. That is precisely the problem Brown wants to chart. With her jeremiad, she seeks to awaken a public to the problem, but she risks becoming its captive.[19] She mentions, in passing, some alternative movements, intimations of possible alternative politics, and this suggests that other things may also be afoot, but she does not give them any real weight, and it is hard to imagine them getting a grip on, much less interrupting, the incredible powers of the new episteme charted by her. These alternative political movements are always there, but, Brown says, they only surface episodically. When they do surface, they politicize what neoliberalism naturalizes or economizes and they do so, often, by way of objects. Inequality was politicized by Occupy, which began with the occupation of a hybrid public/private space, an act quickly followed by the installation of a public library. Our homogenized and industrialized agricultural system undoes food sovereignty and creates food and seed dependency for profit, as Brown notes in an important discussion of Monsanto's operations in Iraq, but this has been resisted too.

The Monsantoization of Iraqi agriculture is just one particularly egregious example of the worldwide industrialization of agriculture, which has been politicized by many activists, though Brown does not note that in detail here. Resistance generates alternative sovereignties gathered around the thingness of food. Slow Food and movements like Food Sovereignty Ireland are instructive examples of resistance to industrial monoculture.[20] Another is the indigenous people in Guatemala who recently won a victory against Monsanto's efforts to patent their seeds, which, because they tend to wander onto other people's farmlands, become like a colonizing force that secures the dictates of Monsanto well beyond the domains of the original buyers of Monsanto's products. In this case, courts, protests, and organizational pressure serve the cause of a sovereignty that Brown laments is lacking on the Left. As one observer says: To the "Mayan people that make up around half of the Guatemalan populous, ownership of the simple corn seed and the freedom to be able to cultivate their own crops mean so much more than simple food freedom."[21] They mean food sovereignty.

Food sovereignty is not just about food; it is about worldviews, action in concert, and public things.[22] Says Lolita Chavez of the Mayan People's Council: "Corn taught us Mayan people about community life and its diversity, because when one cultivates corn one realizes that there is a variety of crops such as herbs and medical plants depending on the corn plant as well. We see that in this coexistence the corn is not selfish, the corn shows us how to resist and how to relate with the surrounding world." To say that the corn is not selfish, and that it gives us instruction, is to say that the corn—a public thing in this context—has agency.

Is the Mayans' activism a mere episode? An expression of a merely infrapolitical experience, as one critic of Latour suggests all such thing-oriented activisms turn out to be?[23] Or might it be evidence of a kind of political action rarely reported in the headlines but nonetheless (or, if we follow James Scott, *therefore*) an important current rival to a momentarily dominant paradigm that claims, falsely, that such rivals have been long since left behind?[24] Food politics depend on their own public things. For example, seed banking is an institutionalized practice, thousands of years old, around which food sovereignty constellates, by which it is periodically (re)generated.[25]

Brown mentions Occupy and other movements in Southern Europe, Turkey, Brazil, and Bulgaria, which "repossessed private as public space, occupied what is owned, and above all, rejected the figure of citizenship reduced to sacrificial human capital and neoliberal capitalism as a life-sustaining sacred power. [All] sought to reclaim the *political* voice hushed by those figures."[26] But none fully succeeded, she says.[27] (Occupy is still at work, however, and it has reset the political agenda. I am not sure how we can yet judge it a success or failure.) Though she notes the various uprisings of 2012 and 2013, Brown does not account for them. How are these neoliberalized subjects acquiring the wherewithal to protest? Why do they risk what they have been taught to think of as their precious human capital? Is it simply that their situation is so bad that they have nothing to lose? Is desperation, rather than the slim hope to which Brown will appeal at the end of her book, actually the source of action? Or do these actors in concert spy alternatives that energize them and give them hope? Not wholesale, perhaps, but piecemeal?

There are other examples to which we could turn for such inspiration. Most revolve around public things—building them, maintaining them, responding to their call. For example, sustainable farming communities, several in the Northeast but also throughout the United States, make real what others might only imagine, or may not be able to imagine.[28] What these farmers have done, many moving from cities to establish rural roots, may look like withdrawal. But these are (also) experiments in living that vivify the imagination and help others to enact alternatives too. Living sustainably and communally on locally grown food, residents of Hardwick, Vermont, model what many elsewhere think is unimaginable. Some of those in the Hardwick area who began committed to building a local sustainable economy went on to become big businesses, it is true (Pete's Greens, for example, exports all around the country now); but the town's model shows the viability of an antigrowth commitment even today when many find irresistible the siren call of growth. The infrastructure of antigrowth—the storefronts, the community meeting places, the farm-to-table delivery systems, and so on—is a public thing.

Another example: the Unist'ot'en Camp's ongoing efforts to prevent oil and gas pipelines from being built on tribal lands in the vicinity of British Columbia, Canada. The pipelines were proposed by Trans Canada (the Pacific Trail Pipeline), which in October 2015 yielded to the tribe, and by Chevron, which, as of May 2016, continues to build in the direction of the camp. As the short film *Holding Their Ground* reports: "The Unist'ot'en never signed a treaty with the Canadian government so, by law, the government or private interests need permission to access their land."[29] This doesn't prevent representatives of Trans Canada's Pacific Trail Pipeline and Chevron from trying. Over and over again. Knowing that the Harper government's antiterror law, C-51, passed in June 2015, "criminalizes interference with critical infrastructure," a tribe member, Freda Huson, turns the charge back against the Harper government and the corporations when she says, brilliantly: "They say they developed C-51 for the purpose of protecting Canada's critical infrastructure projects, and what *we're* doing here is we're protecting *our* critical infrastructure," by which she means the land, itself, and the medicine, berries, fish, and wildlife hunting it provides. When pipeline companies use helicopters to bypass the road checkpoints erected by the Unist'ot'en (an almost weekly occurrence in the summer of 2015), Huson and others jump in their trucks and hurry out to meet them. Asked who they are, the pipeline workers respond: "we're just from Coastal GasLink. We're doing noninvasive testing," as if that absolves them of trespass. But the tribal activists know how invasion begins. Huson says: "Noninvasive testing leads to permits. Permits lead to projects we do not approve of. It's gonna destroy our lands. And the company has already been told you don't have permission to be here. So I'm going to ask you guys to leave," and that day they do.

In July 2015, Chevron representatives appeared at the camp and appealed to the activists' neoliberal rationality, to no avail: "We're here today to talk to you about doing work on your land and are requesting access onto your territory so that Wet'suwet'en people can work and to see benefits from the project. Will you allow access . . . us to access the territory here today?" The reply: "We've already said no to these projects. And that no pipelines will come on our territory and *irregardless if you've got other Wet'suwet'en members working for you* does not gain you access to our territory. . . . You're trying to convince us to give up our way of life so you can reap the benefits for government and investors and . . . while you're throwing crumbs to some of the partners that signed on. . . ."[30] The Chevron representative tries again: "We brought you an offering. We've left some water and some tobacco."

With their choice of objects, the Chevron team evokes the history of white "gifts" to native peoples. The evocation is so explicit that it seems ironic; it is surely meant to provoke the tribe members into reactions that may serve as a pretext to override their rights. But the locals do not take the bait. They have been well trained and are impressively self-disciplined. Huson replies: "No thanks. We've got clean water right here [she points to the fresh water running right alongside them]. That's what we drink and that's [pointing to the "offering" of bottled water] pollution; that's the plastic that adds to the landfill. So you can take your water because we don't want it." This is resistance. But it is not mere resistance. It is resistance to neoliberal rationality on behalf of a vivid and cherished alternative steeped in history, committed to a different future, and vivified in the public things of tribal life: the land, the water, and the herbs, fish, and berries around them, around which their rituals are built. The sovereignty of the tribe and its relationship to public things are constitutively and inextricably intertwined.

Is this not just a clash of things, however? A pipeline versus a river? Gas versus land? As we shall see, Arendt does not allow thingness to be attributed to nature which she thinks is too vital, shapeless, and repetitive, to be thing-like. For her, the natural world lacks the property of object-permanence that makes the human world worldly and human. But, for these tribal activists, nature is not as shapeless and repetitive as Arendt assumes. For them, the natural world is imbued with meaning, myth, and the powers of nurturance, and so it offers, too, the gifts of subject-formation that Winnicott will highlight as part of his object-relations theory. Thus, in the clash between pipeline and river, when both sides claim that what they are pursuing is a public thing ("critical infrastructure"), each is right. One public thing is extractivist and the other is sustainable, one recognizes no limits and the other is sensitive to limitation (hence the mention of landfills). But both *are* public things. Both *are* infrastructure. Pipelines, like the aforementioned sewers, swimming pools, schools, and prisons, create a solidity against which democratic actors committed to environmental preservation may chafe.[31] Other democratic actors may see them—indeed, have seen them!—as unifiers of a nation; this is one task of "critical infrastructure," which was once, and for some still *is*, a nationalizing tool. Think of the national railroads for example: critical transportation infrastructures that were touted as unifiers of the nation in both Canada and the United States.

Pipelines do not just transfer oil or gas. They also underwrite a form of life and give it traction in a world of flux. That is to say, not all public things are "good" from every political angle. Nor can they be all bad, surely. At their best, in their public thingness, they may bring peoples together to act in concert. And even when they are divisive, they provide a basis around which to organize, contest, mobilize, defend, or reimagine various modes of collective being together in a democracy.

Any successful public thing presents us with this problem: the public things that constitute the demos exclude some and privilege others.[32] In the United States, what is called "public" is sometimes white, sometimes black; it is rarely both. Public housing has one racial connotation, public pools, before they were desegregated, another. After public pools were racially integrated, *private* pools became popular among whites, and suburban houses increasingly came with swimming pools in their backyards. The public things of U.S. democracy have been part and parcel of a regime of white supremacy in which equal access to public things—accommodations, travel, parks, streets, wine trains, and more—are denied to people of color. In the context of white supremacy, public things have operated not to equalize people into citizenship but to communicate the terms of a differential citizenship and the frequently subordinating terms of governance and belonging.[33] Thus, when public things *are* democratized, the response of the powerful is often to abandon them. White flight is not just from the urban to the suburban;

it is from the public to the private thing.[34] Privatization and neoliberalization in the United States are part of a racial politics that economistic and
epistemic analyses sideline as merely coincident or irrelevant when they are
likely co-constitutive and certainly coimplicated.

In a way, focusing on the objects rather than the subjects of democracy
might help to highlight anew the inequalities of race and the operations of
white supremacy in the U.S. context. Talk of the demos or the people distinguishes who is in and who is out but it often obscures unequal member-
ships. Talk of public things, however, immediately calls to mind which of
the demos' bodies are policed in public venues and which are assumed to
belong there. American streets are open to free use by some citizens, but
when frequented by others those same streets quickly turn into sites of surveillance or control. Hoodies in malls, homeless people in parks, ethnic minorities in the "wrong" neighborhoods, Muslims going to the mosque, black
protesters sitting at whites-only lunch counters, black teenage girls swimming in a communal pool, dragged out because they are "too loud," then
tackled by grown men in police uniforms, dead bodies left lying in the road.[35]
These incidents, familiar from decades of headlines and history, remind us
how public things are asymmetrically policed, restricted, controlled, these
days without the brazenness of "Whites Only" signs but often no less volu-
bly or effectively. Everyone knows. That is why those excluded or marginalized, and their allies, demand access to them—because that access looks
like citizenship; and it is. But all too often, as soon as access is won, the value
of the public thing or, more accurately, its desirability among whites, goes
down. This is a reason to struggle more mightily for public things, not a
reason to give up on them. It is a reason to invest our best in them, as was
done with New York's Central Park, something everyone wants to be part
of. Democratic sovereignty is an effect, I want to say; public things are its
condition, necessary if not sufficient. They are the basis of democratic flourishing, prods to action in concert.

Perhaps Brown's idea that the Left lacks any interest in sovereignty is
related to the fact that she does not thematize, in their thingness, the public things that do provide some political actors with orientation and cause.
Indeed, the actual existence of movements like the Unist'ot'en Camp's and
other lived alternatives undoes a bit the nearly totalizing picture painted by
Brown, and in particular her book's claims that *homo oeconomicus* has won,

or virtually won. What renders such activist movements unreal by contrast with the supposedly harder, more real realities (often self-proclaimed) of economization?[36] Is it that these movements are good only at reaction, as Brown says, but not at action?[37] Is it that they lack "faith in the powers of knowledge, reason, and will for the deliberate making and tending of our common existence"?[38] Is it that they represent the mere "reform and resistance" whose inadequacies plague a Left dispossessed, Brown says, of any visionary and effective programs and institutions? But maybe "the Left" is the wrong place to look. Recalling no one if not Tocqueville, Brown takes note of the power but also the limits of Occupy and its proclaimed constituency of the 99 percent—which "was not founded on associations of workers, students, consumers, welfare clients, or debtors. Rather, Occupy in fall 2011 was a public coalescing of uprising of solidarities dismantled and citizenries fragmented and dispersed by neoliberal rationality."[39] The old infrastructures of political membership are lacking. They will need to be built. But by whom? And how? The commitments that once informed them have lost out to managerial calculation, Brown says.[40] In place of such calculation, nothing less than sovereignty will do. But the Left seems to lack the appetite or the vision for that.

Acknowledging liberal democracies' implication in "imperial and colonial premises," as well as their many exploitative cruelties and injustices, Brown notes nonetheless that the same liberal democratic form "has also carried—or monopolized, depending on your view—the language and promise of inclusive and shared political equality, freedom, and popular sovereignty." She seems to want to reclaim that, and rightly so: "*What happens to the aspiration for popular sovereignty when the demos is discursively disintegrated? How do subjects reduced to human capital reach for or even wish for popular power? What do radical aspiration for democracy, for humans crafting and controlling their fates together, draw upon . . . ?*"[41] But Brown's claim that we have lost the desire or "aspiration" for sovereignty is resonant in some contexts, less so in others: tribal activists exercise sovereignty in northern British Columbia, Guatemala, and elsewhere. Similarly, the proponents of "food sovereignty," which Brown does mention in the context of her riveting critique of the operations of Monsanto, might have complicated her picture had she considered it in more detail a hundred pages earlier in the book in the context of this lost liberal democratic quest for sovereignty.[42] Sovereignty seems to be not so much lost as dispersed and relocated, growing like a weed in places where it has not been planted before (food sovereignty) or not permitted to grow for a long time (tribal sovereignty). Neoliberalism may "wholly" abandon "the project of individual or collective mastery of existence," deferring instead to markets, but there are other instances of action in concert on the ground, some of them practicing precisely what Brown describes as lost: "collaborative and contestatory human decision making, control over the conditions of existence, planning for the future [and the] deliberate construction of existence through democratic discussion, law, policy."[43] These alternatives are not currently in possession of state institutions and they lack the centralized and accountable power that may be necessary to meet some of our most pressing challenges. But they exist, they understand the predicaments of the moment, and they do not recoil from sovereignty, they seek it on behalf of and in relation to public things that point them to a past and a future.

Brown thinks the takeover of *homo oeconomicus* is complete. Or almost complete; she enters an important caveat: "Alertness to neoliberalism's inconstancy and plasticity cautions against identifying its current iteration as its essential and global truth and against making the story I am telling a teleological one, a dark chapter in a steady march toward end times."[44] But the energy of the book is devoted to tracking the power of neoliberalism, not its limitations. And indeed much of the evidence supports Brown's claim: universities occupied by best practices and benchmarks, the new admin-speak (metrics! learning outcomes!) that evidences many administrators' remove from the spirit of the institutions they are charged with caretaking (though it is only fair to note that these mechanisms began as efforts to exact democratic accountability for schools that failed their students); the Monsantoization of agriculture, which homogenizes and patents food production, obliterating the diversity that is the key to sustainability and local autonomy, and spreading carcinogenic pesticides in its wake. Monsanto's latest seeds are touted as Roundup resistant; this allows the free use of pesticides to kill everything *but* the plant. There is no Roundup resistance for humans, though, nor for the earth and water.

If, as Brown thinks, again with good reason, we have *only homo oeconomicus* to guide us, then we will never work our way out of this mess. And if that is all we have and have become, then singing the praises of public things may seem a paltry response. But Brown herself insists the work is still possible. She says the Left must work to "counter this civilizational despair." The task may be virtually impossible and yet it must be taken on. It is only "this work [that] could afford the slightest hope for a just, sustainable, and habitable future."[45] For me, *public things* are necessary to do this work. They have the power to loosen the grip of Rousseau's paradox of politics, which trains our attention on the people, who are never fully who they need to be in order for democracy to thrive. The focus on the people as such may be precisely the problem, theoretically speaking. It may just pull us back into the orbit of Rousseau's paradox. When we think from the angle of public things, we are switched to questions of orientation and receptivity, from subjectivity to object-ivity, from identity to infrastructure, from membership to world-liness. From a public things perspective, we are more moved first to ask not "who are we?" but "what needs our care and concern?" We are moved out of the realm of infinite cycle (Rousseau's paradox) and into the realm of the more finite and futile, which is the realm of things and the gift (and curse!) of object permanence. Really, more precisely, we are moved into the domain of relations between these two: object *relations*.

Thus, those who want to do the work that "could afford the slightest hope for a just, sustainable, and habitable future" would do well to devote some of their attention to the defense of existing public things, to make them deliver more fully on their promise of true publicness, and to building new ones. For me, public things are like Rousseau's lawgiver who arrives on the scene and finds no *homo politicus* at all. Like that lawgiver, public things, too, have the power to (re)enchant, to interpellate us as a (n often fractious) public in relation to their public thingness and, thus, to break the grip of a seem-ingly intractable paradox so we can rework it, rather than think we have to escape it, knowing we can only fail in the latter effort since the paradox is inescapable. This way of thinking about public things is different from (though indebted to) the varieties of vitalism and thing theory that attribute agency to things and decenter the human. Here the human remains the fo-cus, but things have agency enough to thwart or support human plans or ambitions, and we do well to acknowledge their power and, when appropri-ate, to allow that power to work on us or work to lessen or augment it.[46]

If Brown does not look to public things for their possibly miraculous agency in this context, it may be because she is wary of thing theory's celebratory redistribution of agency to objects at a moment when she thinks humans are lamentably and increasingly deprived of it. This is implied, I think, by Brown's quick dismissal of recent work in posthumanism more generally: "contemporary prescriptive posthumanism expresses the historical conjuncture [of neoliberal reason] and colludes with it."[47] Also, the implication of her reference to Rousseau's paradox of politics is that even if things could issue a call, their call cannot be audible because we are no longer (or not yet) the people we need to be in order to hear it. But sometimes the call breaks through; it starts something where there seems to be nothing.[48]

Or, as in the case of the Unist'ot'en activists, it continues something that was almost crushed but rises up again. Those activists tune into and respond to the berries, the herbs, the salmon, the land, and the rushing waters. Their public things call to them and they respond with sovereignty. The same goes for the Mayans who learn about life from corn and respond to Monsanto with their own brand of sovereignty. It may be that, as with Winnicott's infants and their transitional objects, we depend on public things and they depend on us. And this may mean that Rousseau's paradox, or something like it, is inescapable and irresolvable. But this does not mean we are necessarily defeated by it; there are ways for democratic activists to work within the paradox, to be energized by it.[49] The improbability of the situation leads Arendt to refer to action as a miracle. She also imagines the call that inaugurates action as a kind of speech act. But the call may come from the object world as well.

Take, for example, public telephones.[50] After Hurricane Sandy, pay phones, normally treated as part of New York City's ruined landscape, emerged suddenly to become communications lifesavers, relics with an afterlife. As Ben Cohen noted in the *Wall Street Journal*, "Natural disasters tend to vindicate the pay phone," which is "mounted high and sometimes behind glass stalls [and so] generally remains serviceable during power outages, even amid flooding." Cohen goes on in his article to focus on the only problem would-be users of public telephones faced after Sandy (coin overload), missing the irony of a situation in which the immediate problem is seen as being too much money (coin overload) rather than too little (too little money provided to maintain public things).[51] As a result, the real story—the democratic story of public things—is only intimated but left untold. The real importance of so-called pay phones is that they are, as indeed they were once called, *public* phones, situated on the streets and available to everyone.[52]

Dealing with the effects of flooding, a blackout, and downed cell towers, stormstruck residents of New York City eager to get in touch with friends and loved ones rediscovered the public telephones they had been blithely passing by for years. Said one new user of the old technology quoted by Cohen: "it's funny what's hiding in plain sight . . . it's invisible, but when you need it, it's there."[53] Was she just talking about the phones? What is funny, invisible, but hiding in plain sight is the very idea of public things, things that conjoin people. Shared among users from all kinds of backgrounds, classes, and social locations, the public thing calls out to us, interpellating us as a public. It is all too funny that, in this particular case, the public thing that is calling out to people is in fact a telephone. Will we answer its ring? Many did so, in the aftermath of Sandy, coming together to share the phones, taking messages for strangers, offering change. But with the passing of the emergency, the sound of the public phone became less and less audible.

We might see the quaintness of the old fashioned phones as a synecdoche for the quaintness, in our mostly neoliberal context, of publicness itself. I imagine that is how it would look to Brown, and it does so to me, too, a lot of the time. But the public phone harbors another possibility, as well. We could say that the emergency of the storm brought out a kind of craving for the public thing, the thing that hides in plain sight, but when you need it, it's there. This is different from the mass consumerist need to all be in love with the same private object—the newest iPhone, say—and to have one, of which there are millions. When people own objects privately, they experience the objects' personal and perhaps fetishistic magic (otherwise why would we bother owning anything?) but privately owned objects lack the political magic that is my focus in these lectures. That is why Arendt says about such things that "this enlargement of the private, the enchantment, as it were, of a whole people, does not make it public . . . for while the public realm may be great, it cannot be charming precisely because it is unable to harbor the irrelevant."[54] Thus, it is not exactly that objects lose their thingness in neoliberalism (they may or may not); the concern here is that they lose their *political* thingness. That political thingness is as precious and necessary for the body politic as is the personal magic of the transitional object for the individual in Winnicott's object-relations theory. It is not that the object exerts a personal magic on all of us in common, but that all of us in common get our very sense of commonness from the object. We may think this happens in relation to objects like the iPhone, and it may; we cannot rule that out. But the consumer need for such commodities—the fetish—is more like the ruin, the remnant, of the democratic desire to constellate affectively around shared objects, public things. The ruin testifies to a not quite lost past; might it also bode a possible future?

Sometimes the ruin speaks. The desire for a democracy of public things has been in recent decades rechanneled into commercial formats, but it is not extinguished. The signs are there: The desire remains, the aspiration is alive, but they require redirection and sustenance.

In the aftermath of Sandy, there were demands for better cell phone towers to secure coverage in emergencies. But no one called for better support for the public telephones that served the public so ably this time. Why not? This response (the response of Brown's *homo oeconomicus*, undoubtedly) is rather like the decision to build more roads for cars a century ago, in place of investing in public transportation. But the ruin calls for a different response. Why not commit instead to preserve the pay phones in appreciation of the fact that the ones in New York City, that most palimpsest-like of all cities, seem miraculously to work? (But not only miraculously, or at least not miraculously in the usual sense: Someone has been tending to them, maintaining the critical communications infrastructure of the city undeterred by the fact that most city residents have withdrawn from it, preferring their own private communications devices, until they fail.[55]) Why not turn pay phones from relics of a lost past into the stable new infrastructure of a possible new future of public things?[56] True, in such a scenario public phones may become mere emergency phones, which would be ironic since "emergency" has fast become the only public thing left to us. On the other hand, though, as long as we have *a* public thing, the space is arguably open for the return of other public things. In the ruins of public things, the return of public things remains imaginable and realizable. Almost.

Public phones hide in plain sight, but when we need them they are there. (This is how Winnicott characterizes the "good enough mother"—invisible, but when you need her, she's there.) We just need to answer their call. And if we do not answer, they may not be there for us the next time. For Brown, presumably, the loss of public things is part and parcel of the loss

of a language of publicness, a loss of citizenship as such, the loss of a politics at the (invisible) hands of economics. But, in my view, public things
stand out as a point worth insisting upon, something that must not be allowed to become part of the morass of despair. Their thingness still enchants, even as their publicness is under pressure. Anyone who has visited a
national park can attest to this.[57]

Brown ends her book with a kind of appeal to something like what Jonathan Lear calls "radical hope" (though Brown's is a "slight" hope) or to Hanna
Pitkin's "just do it."[58] For Lear, radical hope springs from the very abyss in
which despair might take root. Such hope is unaccountable and it presses us
to act without knowing what the future may bring, without a plan, without
a program: blind. Brown recalls Lear when she closes her book worried about
despair (*désespoir*: hopelessness). But Lear, unaware perhaps, offers us something other than radical hope. He does not single it out for attention but in
his portrait of the Crow chief Plenty Coups, whom he admires for his capacity to act hopefully in the context of catastrophe, Lear reports Plenty
Coups' profound dedication to establishing new public things for a tribe
whose old ones had been destroyed. Lear's Plenty Coups, like a Rousseauian
lawgiver, understood the power of public things and was committed to providing them for his people who had somehow survived world-ending white
conquest and had to face the impossible task of rebuilding their world.

Having noted public things' occlusion of past injustices, thefts, inju-
ries, and their ongoing harms, we must note another problem too: insofar
as they conjoin us, public things may also implicate us in causes and actions in
which we would rather not be implicated, for political or moral reasons. In
the context of neoliberalism, we hear about "opting out."[59] A clerk working
in a Kentucky public office that grants marriage licenses refuses to serve
gay couples after the Supreme Court prohibits such discrimination.[60] Hobby
Lobby and others have sought exemption from participation in the new U.S.
national healthcare system, since they object to being a vehicle through which
birth control is delivered to women.[61] We have seen in recent years many
such efforts to opt out of part or all of the public thing (which is then re-
named in a way that marks it as a partial, not public, thing: "Obamacare,"
gay marriage). Those opting out invoke reasons that sound quite like Bernard
Williams's well-known motto for integrity over compliance: "Not through
me." What Williams means is that when a society pursues ends with which

I—as a moral agent of integrity—am constitutively at odds, I am not necessarily morally bound to devote myself to opposing them, politically, but I may be morally bound to refuse to be a vehicle through which such ends are pursued. There is a difference, however, between Williams's "not through me" and the neoliberal practice of opting out, and we may put it like this: Opting out postulates a kind of membership in the public thing that is rooted in buy-in. Buy-in is a very different relationship to public things than the constitutive, enchanted affiliation and desire explored here. Buy-in postulates something more like a prior purchase that can be returned when we decide we don't want it after all.[62] There are other differences as well.

Williams nearly anticipates the case of the Kentucky clerk when he imagines the example of a pacifist chemist, George, who has to decide whether or not to take a badly needed job in a chemical weapons factory. Williams argues that even a badly needed job is not reason enough for moral subjects to put their integrity at risk, which is surely what happens when we go daily to work in a place whose mission is deeply at odds with our fundamental moral commitments. Notably, here, "opting out" consists in *refusing* the job, not in performing the job in some sabotaging way (an option considered by George, but ultimately dismissed by him in Williams's telling). This is quite different from the Kentucky case where the officeholder holds on to the job that requires performance of an act she says she considers morally repugnant. Perhaps the job is badly needed. But perhaps, given her celebrity-seeking behavior during and after the initial controversy, the clerk held onto the job precisely in order to be able to refuse to serve an already beleaguered minority, even though (or, more likely, because) such service is now legally required. Perhaps she chose a *political* alternative, not moral cleanliness but political sabotage, the very alternative that Williams's George dismisses as unlikely to add up to anything and likely to undermine his own integrity.[63]

Either way, this is not an instance of Bernard Williams's considered "not through me." The Kentucky clerk here opts out but declines to give up the job that puts her in this compromised (from her point of view) situation. True, the chemist has to decide whether or not to take the job, while the clerk has the job and would have to decide to give it up when its obligations change due to a Court decision. So there is some difference there insofar as inertia protects the moral integrity of the chemist but betrays that of the clerk. But inertia is not a factor in Williams's account, nor should it be. It may be a part of the story but it is not a reason. From Williams's perspective, the clerk ought to leave the job but, instead, she refuses to leave the job while refusing to do the job as is now required. We could see this as civil disobedience, or as a politics of conscience, as she and her supporters certainly want us to, but such cases of conscience and disobedience are usually about responsibilities that cannot be avoided or evaded, such as serving in the military when there is a military draft. In such cases, the subject of integrity *cannot* simply refuse the job; s/he is forced into criminality by such a choice or into exceptionality, if there is allowance for conscientious objection. Still, such refusal is clearly what Williams would prefer over the daily erosion of moral agency and the destruction of self that are bound to result from immersion and implication in ends we judge morally repugnant.

There is something to stay with here, however. There is much to criticize in the Kentucky clerk case and in the case of Williams's imagined pacifist chemist. But both examples usefully press on us acknowledgment of the fact that public things involve us in matters not of our own choosing. This is a fact in their favor, insofar as this trait works to weaken the Rousseauian paradox of politics. But it is also a problem, of course, insofar as their claimed universality is never truly so (hence the move in the last twenty years by Nancy Fraser and others to talk about "multiple publics"), and insofar as they may not only enchant us into equality but also implicate and enlist us in policies and actions we abhor. The Winnicottian holding environment, we may note, is a place where we are, as he puts it, "handled" and "held." In political life, we are handled into crimes and held alongside injustices, and we should object to that. Conscientious objection is one safety valve for such situations, a limitation on the expectation of subscription, an allowance for principled, costly disavowal or disidentification.[64] But the conscientious objector and the opt-out are importantly different. The objector, with her objection, claims membership *in* the public thing, but the opt-out can opt out because her relationship to the public thing is transactional, perpetually subject to (re) evaluation.[65]

In the remaining two lectures I will be looking at the constitutive powers of public things and how we relate to them in democratic settings. In Lecture Two, I argue that Arendt herself can be read as a kind of object-relations theorist, given that she granted to object permanence the important capacity to stabilize a world fit for human inhabitation. The argument develops out of a new reading of *The Human Condition* in which the Work section of the book—the relatively neglected part of the book that details, among other things, the functions and powers of things—is key. Read with Winnicott, Arendt emerges as a thinker keenly committed to the power of thingness to stabilize the flux of nature and the contingency of action. Things, on her account, gift us with permanence. But the relations she thinks are most fundamental are human ones, and when she turns to focus on those in the Action section of her book, objects drop out of view. Winnicott helps generate an appreciation for the important place of things in Arendt's work but he also introduces a supplement: a kind of thing-agency that goes beyond Arendt's account. He knows we are born into a world of things, from which we learn and to which we respond, and he does not underrate their power to mediate and enable relations among persons.

It is notable that Arendt and Winnicott both developed their ideas about object permanence in the context of World War II. Winnicott worked with children orphaned or separated from their families by the London bombings. Arendt was, herself, a war-tossed Jew who saw firsthand how people who were denationalized, deprived of their civic belonging, were also deprived of the belongings that betokened their humanity. For her, as we shall see, things have the power to humanize. These are points made, as is well known, in her study of the conditions and conduct of European anti-Semitism, imperialism, and totalitarianism in *The Origins of Totalitarianism*. My claim is that they may well inform what many have until now taken to be her merely phenomenological account of Work in *The Human Condition*.

In Lecture Three, I turn from the catastrophe of war that is in the background of these particular works by Arendt and Winnicott to the world-ending catastrophes that are in the foreground of Jonathan Lear's book *Radical Hope* and Lars von Trier's film *Melancholia*. Both Lear and von Trier explore the repertoires of resilience on which people draw when facing world-ending calamities. We may read their work as parables of climate catastrophe, perhaps, or of the end of capitalism, or even of the world-endingness of capitalism. If both explore or imagine the experience of world-ending, is that, perhaps, for reasons suggested by Fredric Jameson's observation in *The Seeds of Time*: "It seems to be easier for us today to imagine the thoroughgoing deterioration of the earth and of nature than the breakdown of late capitalism; perhaps that is due to some weakness in our imaginations"?[66]

This connection between capitalism and catastrophe is thematized in von Trier's *Melancholia*, as we shall see, but what is important is that the film depicts resignation but does not traffic in it. Many viewers reported a sense of euphoria after seeing the film and certainly both von Trier and Lear seek to strengthen our imaginations. From both, we may also learn about the importance to us now of a democracy of public things, though von Trier, I will argue, goes further than Lear to underline the necessary conditions of action *in concert*, which include not just hope but also play.

Perhaps not coincidentally, both also feature adolescents faced with dilemmas of maturation and progress in a world that is inhospitable to their needs. Thwarted adolescence was one of Winnicott's own areas of interests, as it happens. He saw the thwarting as a sign of popular discomfort with the emerging autonomy and power of young people, and he worried about how, in the United States, where postwar culture demanded that youth be compliant rather than autonomous, adolescent transgression was too quickly criminalized. Winnicott did not address the racial and class makeup of these asymmetries in the United States but demands for conformity and compliance have always been asymmetrically enforced in the United States. Some adolescents are allowed their waywardness, and others are criminalized in anticipation of their perceived likeliness to become wayward lawbreakers one day soon. From some, compliance is expected. From others, autonomy is assumed. Some are seen as criminals in the making, others as youth sowing wild oats.

If public things have a certain Winnicottian magic, it is not that they can magically heal such social divisions or blind us to racial hierarchies. It is that they furnish a world in which we encounter others, share the experience of being part of something that is larger than ourselves, and work with others, acting in concert, to share it, to democratize access to it, to better it, to desegregate it, to maintain it. A politics of public things is committed to the daily practice of preserving, augmenting, and contesting the qualities that make public things both "public" and "things." Public things are things around which we constellate, and by which we are divided and interpellated into agonistic democratic citizenship. They are not innocent or pure. They are political.

Care and Concern: Arendt with Winnicott

I turn now to look at "things" in Hannah Arendt's work, in connection with D. W. Winnicott's object relations discussed in Lecture One and now, in more detail, here. My aim in this lecture is to generate a lexicon for a political theory of public things that we can then use in Lecture Three. Reading Arendt with Winnicott here, in Lecture Two, I argue that there is a case to be made for seeing Arendt as a kind of object-relations theorist whose concepts, along with Winnicott's, call attention to the centrality of public things to democratic forms of life. Winnicott is interested in the psychological development of the individual and Arendt in political action in concert, but his concepts are useful to thinking about collectivities and public things, and not necessarily in developmental terms. Moreover, when Arendt explores categories of experience and sensation (privacy, needs, pain), her claims seem idiosyncratic and often confound her readers: Winnicott's psychoanalytic perspective helps make sense of them. Arendt does not join Winnicott in thinking of objects or things in relation to fantasy, nor does she explicitly consider their role in subject-formation. Still, reading Arendt with Winnicott helps us see that she does attribute great powers to things: They transform the natural and human world into a stable, durable environment "fit for human habitation."[1]

When we read Arendt together with Winnicott, we see how things are shapers (Arendt) and even sources (Winnicott) of our capacity to care for the world. Some of what Arendt says about things can be extended usefully to public things, which help stabilize the common world and provide specific points of orientation for action in concert. The same is true for Winnicott's "transitional objects"; like them, so too *public* things may materially and symbolically transition us between private and public, and mediate our relations with others and with ourselves as subjects and citizens. Winnicott and Arendt do not converge entirely, though. He values the magic of things in their everydayness. Arendt insists such enchantment is neither quotidian nor desirable. For her, the gift of things has more to do with their facticity than with fantasy, though I will argue that in practice these are harder to distinguish than she assumes. Noting how the facticity of things is inseparable from our fantasies and psychic investments, a political theory of public things turns to Winnicott to counterbalance Arendt's account. And Arendt's account, in turn, counterbalances Winnicott's by suggesting that object relating is not just about individuals in a maternally secured holding environment, but also about collectivities in democratically secured political holding environments. Public things—objects of both facticity and fantasy—underwrite our collective capacities to imagine, build, and tend to a common world collaboratively. Read together, each of these thinkers generates new insights about the other and helps to foreground the circular dependence of the capacities for care (Arendt) or concern (Winnicott) on public things and vice versa.[2]

The central text here, in Lecture Two, is *The Human Condition*, in which Arendt prizes things for their capacity to lend permanence to the world. For Arendt, things are part of what provides us with a world in which to move and they provide the friction of finitude that limits or thwarts but also drives human care for the world. Arendt says at the very beginning of *The Human Condition*: "The *vita activa*, human life insofar as it is actively engaged in doing something, is always rooted in a world of men and of man-made things. . . ."[3] Men and Things. For Arendt, the *world* of world care includes not just a "'physical . . . in-between'" (Things) but also a "'subjective in-between'" made up of "'deeds and words'" (Men).[4] Together, these make up what Arendt calls the "common world," whose distinctive feature is that it outlasts any one human life: it "is what we have in common not only with those who live with us, but also with those who were here before and with those who will come after us."[5] If I keep the focus on things, and not the common world in this lecture, it is because, as we shall see, the "things" and the "men" turn out to be coimplicated in ways we can better apprehend from the perspective of object relations. It is also because public things are somewhere between Arendt's "men" and "things." They are the "common world" in Arendt, and they are among the necessary conditions of democracy here.

Arendt gives several examples of things that lend their artifice to the human world. Shoes, tables, craftwork, sculpture, art, and more are made by us but exist independently of us, and in their durability and permanence they serve as sources of orientation for us. The world "consists of things produced by human activities; but the things that owe their existence exclusively to men nevertheless constantly condition their human makers."[6] We vest Things with meaning, but Things also anchor and orient us, she says.

Although the particulars in their accounts of object permanence differ, Arendt is close here to D. W. Winnicott's object-relations theory. As we shall see, her commitment to natal action in concert converges with his commitment to what he calls "liveness." Her "care" for the world converges with his "concern" for others.[7] These key terms, object permanence, action, natality, liveness, care, and concern, are the building blocks of a theoretical, conceptual vocabulary upon which a political theory of public things can draw.

Bringing Arendt and Winnicott together may seem forced, or at least unlikely, since Arendt hated psychoanalysis for its effort to make a science of human behavior, and Winnicott never attended to political theory.[8] But Arendt was an acute psychological observer, especially when thinking about the desire of the marginalized and the poor for social acceptance (or visibility) and the human need for durability. And Winnicott was not your typical psychoanalytic theorist. Although he talked about developmental stages, he always insisted these recur throughout our lifetimes. Although he theorized the patterns and "processes of maturation," he was alert to the quirky and individual styles of people's negotiations of these processes, and so he almost

never comes across as formulaic.[9] Finally, he was prone to delightful obser-
vations like this: "one is at a music hall and on the stage come the dancers
trained to liveness. One can say here is anal control, here is masochistic
submission to discipline, and here is a defiance of the superego. Sooner or
later one adds: here is LIFE."[10] This life-affirming declaration of the life-
effacing impact of certain kinds of behavioral and psychological explanation fits perfectly with Arendt's oft-stated critique of the reductionism of
the behavioral sciences.

These two mid-century thinkers, both humanists, share a hard-earned,
war-tossed appreciation of the importance of stable, worldly *things* to our
capacity to achieve stability, integrity, and adhesion to things and to each
other. In Winnicott, these *things* are transitional objects (the blanket, the
teddy bear). In Arendt, they are the durable products of Work or fabrica-
tion that lend their "tangibility" to the human world.[11] Arendt emphasizes
"publicness" in ways Winnicott does not: the "common world can survive
the coming and going of generations only to the extent that it appears in
public."[12] Winnicott, by contrast, emphasizes the importance of the "holding environment," secured by a "good enough" (m)other, in which we are
cared for and develop capacities for individuation, experimentation, adaptation, concern, and collaboration. For both, things are key here, to trans-
temporal continuity, for Arendt, and as transitional objects in the holding
environment, for Winnicott. For both, the space or domain of the individual's emergence is a kind of in-between (Arendt) or between (Winnicott).

I turn now to look at Arendt's *The Human Condition* from an object-
relations perspective with the aim of underscoring the centrality of things
and thingness to her work in that text. I seek not simply to translate her arguments into Winnicott's language, but with his concepts to reopen some
old debates in the Arendt scholarship, and see her work afresh. In the last
twenty years or more, Arendt has been enlisted by liberals, deliberative demo-
crats, and radicals who see in her account of Action some authorization for
the proceduralism, deliberation, or equality they value. In a way, her work
is like a microcosm of the democratic theory situation outlined in Lecture
One, in which the fundamental role of public things in democratic life has
been effaced or neglected for quite some time.[13] Winnicott's object-relations
theory helps to correct that, as we shall see. And Arendt's references to care
give us a reason to consider Winnicott's treatment of "concern" not just as

a contribution to a theory of child development but also as a contribution to a political theory of public things.

In *The Human Condition*, Arendt distinguishes three domains of human activity—Labor, Work, and Action—and gives a phenomenological account of them, specifying what properly belongs to each; each has different activities, mentalities, and temporalities. Labor and Action could not be more different, but when viewed from the angle of vision provided by Work, they can be seen to mirror each other in several key respects.

Labor is the domain of life-preservation and consumption where life is mere life: biological and causally determined. The activities here are typically ceaseless and repetitive. They would include things like cooking, cleaning, farming, diaper-changing, and tending to people's health and illness.[14] No matter how well we do these things, they always need to be done again and again and what is at stake in doing them is mere life itself. The subject of Labor is *animal laborans* and muteness is our creaturely condition in that domain.[15] In Action, by contrast, life is not merely biological and mortal; it is natal and immortalizable. Action is the domain of inaugural speech, meaning-making, and political action in concert among equals. People, governed not by causality but contingency, perform great acts in concert and contribute to the world's (wide) web of human relations and meaning. In Labor, we live under the sign of necessity, but in the realm of Action we experience freedom. Anything can happen.[16]

Positioned between Labor and Action, Work serves as a stable partner for each of the other two. Indeed, a close reading of *The Human Condition* shows that the section on Work is the spine and soul of the book, though few Arendt scholars have noted this.[17] This domain underwrites and secures the other two, which are both impermanent, each in its own way. Labor is subject to the ceaseless eternality of bio-reproduction and Action to the uncertain immortality of great acts. Both depend on Work to offset the vicissitudes of their unique temporalities. The fabricated objects of Work provide shelter from the storms that Labor must weather. "Without defending himself against the natural processes of growth and decay, the *animal laborans* could never survive."[18] *Homo faber*, the subject of Work, fabricates the hammers, nails, and ploughs that ease the burdens of Labor.[19] And he creates the poems, memorials, sculptures, and histories that shelter the memories created by Action. Work's things reify and extend the vital renown of the political actor and stabilize the web of meanings in which we live and into which we may act. Work provides the actor with the infrastructure of secular immortality.

Work's products are objects and their contribution to the ceaseless repetition (Labor) and uncertain flux (Action) of the human world is nothing less than what Winnicott calls "object permanence." As Arendt herself says, things contribute something unique to the human condition. "The ideals of homo faber, the fabricator of the world . . . are permanence, stability, and durability."[20] These ideals serve the other two domains of human life underwriting both survival (in Labor's cyclical time) and immortality (in Action's linear time).[21]

In psychological terms, the domain of Labor is immersive.[22] Attentive above all to survival, and premised on our utter similarity to each other, Labor does nothing to secure personal boundaries and so the problem posed by it is how to separate or individuate from others. Labor is also ceaseless, and so another problem posed by it is how to interrupt or punctuate its ceaseless temporality. From an object-relations perspective, we could say that we need durable objects to give definition to persons, lest we be consumed by Labor and remain always and everywhere *animal laborans*. Arendt's aim here is to identify the conditions under which both persons and time can be bounded and defined. Work and its objects help with this. Similarly, in psychological terms, the realm of Action poses challenges of its own. Premised on our singularity, Action confronts us not just with the problem of how to individuate (this is well known) but also with the problem of how collaboratively to create and sustain human connection in time. We do so by establishing not just durability, which is Work's corrective for Labor, but immortality, which is Work's gift to Action: the memorials, statuary, and poems that Work provides. These also relieve to some extent our exposure both to the timeless, inhuman eternity of nature in Labor and even the mortal finitude of Work.

I think a case can be made for thinking of Arendt's category of Work as a kind of Winnicottian "holding environment" that provides the objects that enable us to transition from the needs-based domain of Labor into the more individuating experience of Action. Arendt's way of talking about Labor, Work, and Action is phenomenological and spatial, not developmental, but if we think of her three domains in developmental terms for just a moment we can see more readily how the move from Labor to Action follows a recognizable Winnicottian trajectory from immersion to individuation (though Winnicott himself says these changes recur throughout a life and are not connected only to early stages of development). The aim here is not to conflate Arendt's political theory with Winnicott's psychological one but to gain some insight into both by appreciating an important convergence between them and the divergences, too: both Arendt and Winnicott see object relating as a sort of conceptual (not necessarily developmental) hinge between needs and independence (infantlike/need-oriented and individuated/mature/public) and both characterize the more mature or individuated state as a "between" (Winnicott) or an "in-between" (Arendt).[23]

In Winnicott's account of object relations, however, the transitional objects that enable us to move from one developmental stage to the next are things like a baby's blanket or teddy bear.[24] These are not Arendt's type of example, at all. She is much more drawn to the human traits she *metaphorizes* as "natality" than she is interested in actual children.[25] Winnicott's work with children puts some flesh, as it were, onto her abstract concept of natality, and this highlights their overlaps, which are striking: Arendt sounds quite like Winnicott on infant development when she talks about the human need to transform "the desperate longing of needs" into things that "are fit to enter the world."[26] The device of that transformation, she says, is "reification." This is Winnicott's device as well for stabilizing the chaos of feelings into a form of stable subjectivity: hence, the "transitional object."[27]

Winnicott's objects are called "transitional" because they play a key role in transitional stages of development and because infants rely on them to make the transition from dependence on the mother-figure to more independent capacities to play without her. Like the things of Arendt's Work, Winnicott's transitional objects are autonomous, resilient, possessed of permanence, and not prone to obsolescence, though they are not immune, either, to wear and tear. Even those who have never heard of Winnicott are familiar with these ideas of his. We nod or smile in recognition at references to terms like blankie, na-na, or teddy. These fabrics, pacifiers, and stuffed animals are the enchanted source of magical comfort to infants of a certain age or stage of development. Infants are desolate when such objects are lost, distraught when they are damaged (or, God forbid, *laundered*) and relieved or blissful when they are found, recovered, or restored. In these cases, the object is not *obviously* magical. It is often rather disgusting. Infants provide the magic that makes the object special, imbuing the object with the comfort, security, or calm that is then, in turn, bestowed on them by their precious, precious thing. "Transitional objects have a physical existence, and at the same time they are pressed into the service of inner psychic reality."[28] No one but the infant can appoint or designate a certain blanket as the blankie, the fabric that soothes. Such a relationship, an object relation, can be solicited by an adult, but in the end the psychic investment and the choice of object are the infant's to make in one of his or her earliest acts of spontaneity and creativity.

The emphasis in Winnicott is on the capacity of the transitional object to withstand the changing moods of the child, the rage and the love, both of which can be destructive. Although, as I have noted, Arendt does not talk about children or maturation in *The Human Condition*, it is this same test in her work, not just of durability but also, and in particular, of independence from human mood or appetite that fits some things into the category of Work, where humans fabricate objects, rather than Labor, where humans consume nature's offerings and reproduce them for further consumption in the cyclical time of the seasons. Arendt herself makes something like Winnicott's point when she comments on the thing-like properties of shoes that "survive even for a considerable time the changing moods of their owner. Used or unused, they will remain in the world for a certain while unless they are wantonly destroyed."[29]

In Winnicott, however, the object survives not just the changing moods of the child, but also, precisely, the child's wanton destructiveness. Such wanton destruction is always a possibility since, in Winnicott's world, we are the subjects of ugly feelings (to borrow Sianne Ngai's title). We are also creatures of fantasy. Sometimes, even often, we destroy the objects we use and they survive. We fantasize destroying them, and they survive. We love them for this and in loving them, we acquire some of their resilience; it rubs off on us, as it were. This is the magic of object relations. The object is destroyed (in fantasy) but it lives on, materially, and its effects and powers radiate out to us.

This is a step further than Arendt herself goes. Since Winnicott explains the idea of the thing's destruction and survival by saying that it entails a shift in focus from object *relations* to object *use*, we may think that Arendt is perhaps best seen as theorizing, in Winnicott's terms, object relations more than object use. In fact, however, it is most accurate to say that she is think-ing in the Work section of *The Human Condition* about the object's contri-bution in object relations, but not about the subject's, whose fantasies play a key role in this process on Winnicott's account:

> This change (from relating to usage) means that the subject destroys the object. From here *it could be argued by an armchair philosopher that* there is therefore no such thing in practice as the use of an object: *if the object is external, then the object is destroyed by the subject.* Should the philosopher come out of his chair and sit on the floor with his patient, however, he will find that there is an *intermediate position.* In other words, he will find that after "subject relates to object" comes "subject destroys object" (as it becomes external); and then may come "object survives destruction by the subject." But there may or may not be survival. A new feature thus arrives in the theory of object-relating. *The subject says to the object: "I destroyed you," and the object is there to receive the communication.* From now on the subject says: "Hullo object!" "I destroyed you." "I love you." "You have value for me because of your survival of my destruction of you." "While I am loving you I am all the time destroying you in (unconscious) fantasy." *Here fantasy begins for the individual. The subject can now use the object that has survived.* It is important to note that it is not only that the subject destroys the object because the object is placed outside the area of omnipotent control. *It is equally significant to state this the other way round and to say that it is the destruction of the object that places the object outside the area of the subject's omnipotent control. In these ways the object develops its own autonomy and life, and (if it survives) contributes-in to the subject, according to its own properties.*[30]

If it survives, the object "contributes-in to the subject, according to its own properties." Note how, for Winnicott, the capacity to survive destruc-tion is both a trait we grant *to* the object (in reality or fantasy) and a trait we acquire *from* objects, by way of a kind of (unnamed) transference. Durability or permanence is what the autonomous object "*contributes-in to the subject, according to its own properties,*" underwriting a self that is collected, capable of creativity, spontaneity, and liveness.

For Winnicott, the capacity of objects to constitute a stable world de-rives not solely from their solidity, as Things, nor even from our fabrica-tion of them. These are the suggestions of Arendt's phenomenology. The stability of Winnicott's transitional objects derives from their enchanted condensation of, and entry into, complicated sets of affective relations under-written by certain affective, relational environments, and ultimately also by fantasy.[31] This may be true of Arendt's things as well, though she does not contemplate the possibility. She attributes their durability to their physical properties, and not to our attachment to them or to their meaning for us. Thus, things are more circular in Winnicott than in Arendt (though they are circular for her too: we make things and things condition our existence, she says[32]). Like so much else in Winnicott, this circularity situates us in some connection with an in-between and a paradox: the relationship between person and thing (in-between), and the undecidability (or circularity) of the thing as found and/or invented. "The baby creates the object, but the object was there waiting to be created and to become a cathected object," Winnicott says,[33] warning against intellectualizing or resolving the paradox: "It is possible to resolve the paradox, but the price of this is the loss of the value of the paradox itself."[34] The paradox depends on parental reticence: "It is a matter of agreement between us and the baby that we will never ask the question: 'Did you conceive of this or was it presented to you from without?'"[35] A certain phenomenological agnosticism is a postulate of Winnicott's object-relations theory. It is better not to know and better not to need to know.[36] Leaving things unexplained, or, as Wittgenstein would say, allowing explanation to run out, respects the vital powers of meaning and fantasy.

Fantasy, affect, enchantment, are less of a theme in Arendt (which will surprise no one who knows her work) but they do come up at one point in *The Human Condition*, precisely in relation to things and the tendency of some people in some circumstances to attach to them:

> Since the decay of their once great and glorious public realm, the French have become masters in the art of being happy among "small things," within the space of their own four walls, between chest and bed, table and chair, dog and cat and flowerpot, extending to these things a care and tenderness which, in a world where rapid industrialization constantly kills off the things of yesterday to produce today's objects, may even appear to be the world's last purely humane corner. This enlargement of the private, the enchantment, as it were, of a whole people, does not make it public. . . . For while the public realm may be great, it cannot be charming precisely because it is unable to harbor the irrelevant.[37]

The issue here, for Arendt, is not just the outsized affection—"care and tenderness"—lavished on tiny things in a desperate attempt at happiness in a diminished situation.[38] It is also the occasion of that, which is twofold: the fall of the French public realm, which Arendt suggests had once offered a kind of lastingness, and the changes in object-production that do so no longer. Here something has gone terribly wrong with the care that Arendt normally admires because Work and Action are no longer providing a world to care *for*. Parisians—and all of us—are left with things incapable of repaying an affective investment that is more symptom than charm, as we seek out a last refuge of a disappearing humaneness. If the objects here *contribute—in according their own properties* to the subject, then what they contribute is a certain diminution (a theme to which I return in Lecture Three). Rather than enhance, they diminish the subject, and her powers to care for the world are diminished as well. This is in part because she is caring for the wrong sorts of things (*bric-a-brac*) and in part because those things are in the wrong sort of context: inside four walls, not in a great public realm; in the context of industrialized production and not in relation to the kinds of Work that makes things that are meant to last. For Arendt, the Parisian practice of care for the world has gone inside where it cares for what it can and for what is left. This is a world-ending development for her, the opposite of the inaugural experience of Action she celebrates.[39]

Winnicott may provide a useful counterbalance here to Arendt since he would be less quick to assume an unhealthy attachment to things, as such, in the Parisian situation. Where Arendt sees fetish, he might well counsel us to assume healthy attachments to transitional objects. Whether or not that is the case would very much depend on individual details in individual cases and not on wholesale generalizations about "Parisians." Yet, there is something compelling about what Arendt says here, and that is because of what I take to be her interest in the *democratic* holding environment, not the maternal one to which Winnicott attends. We might even follow Arendt's lead and speculate that one reason Americans these days seem so caught up with television shows about home design is that they do not know how to care for the world. In fact, they have been prevented from doing so, through an elaborate array of regulations, policings, and surveillance that discourage people from joining together to act in concert, and by the growth of American power to such an extent that it is difficult to know how or where to intervene in it, though many still do make the effort, as I pointed out in Lecture One. The problem in the United States is not what Arendt describes as the disappearance of the public realm, but the many explicit announcements that it is closed for business.

So, in Arendt's terms, the American love of the world becomes a love of home. Instead of Parisian minimization, we have gone for maximization. Energies that might have been spent on community work find their outlets in new kitchens, new houses, new paint colors, and so on.[40] These are not the only two choices, however, by way of which to understand our relations to things, public and private. I think it is fair to say that Arendt and Winnicott would agree that, somewhere between dissociation and displaced hyper-attachment, there is a third option: healthy attachment to transitional objects in various holding environments can charm individuals and publics into collecting themselves together for the world.[41] Both thinkers do take seriously the role of private things in private spaces to provide the orientation and belonging that fill fundamental needs and generate the capacity for care (Arendt) or concern (Winnicott) about the world. Both would also have to acknowledge that acting out of care for the world can certainly occur in the absence of these conditions, as when people deprived of them rise up to protest injustice—for example, the marches of the undocumented in the mid-2000s and the work of the Dreamers and others since on behalf of amnesty and immigration reform.[42]

Once again, Arendt and Winnicott, writing in two very different registers, emphasizing different considerations in relation to things, nonetheless converge. Arendtian "care" is Winnicott's "concern," and both prioritize action or the opportunity to contribute as essential to the development of the capacity in question. Winnicott underscores the dependence of the child on the caregiver's provision of opportunities to act on concern in the holding environment, while Arendt writes on behalf of preserving opportunities to act in concert in the diminishing public spaces of the late modern world.

In "The Capacity for Concern," Winnicott explains that concern, by which he means "the fact that the individual *cares*, or *minds*, and both feels and accepts responsibility," is a healthy trait connected to the feeling of being useful.[43] In order to get to this stage, the infant has to achieve ambivalence ("the simultaneous love-hate experience" whose "enrichment and refinement . . . leads to the emergence of concern").[44] Winnicott explains this ambivalence by introducing a distinction between two aspects of infant care, in personified terms: the "object-mother" and the "environment-mother." He draws the distinction with some trepidation: "I have no wish to invent names that become stuck and eventually develop a rigidity and an obstructive quality," he says. But it is good he took the risk. His distinction between the object-mother and the environment-mother maps well onto Arendt's distinction between Labor and Work, and presses us to a new assessment of these as well as to a new appreciation of the conditions of care and concern in these two thinkers.

The two aspects of mother-care, Winnicott explains, "describe the vast difference that there is for the infant between two aspects of infant-care, the mother as object, or owner of the part-object that may satisfy the infant's urgent needs, and [the environment-mother] the mother as the person who wards off the unpredictable and who actively provides care in handling and in general management."[45] The contribution of the environment-mother is to fail immediately to anticipate the child's needs and in so doing to provide him/her with what s/he needs most: independence.[46] The infant makes very different use of each of these two, directing aggression at the object-mother and affection at the environment-mother, from whom the infant does not just take but with whom the infant also collaborates and to whom s/he can contribute something. Concern enters the child's life as a possibility when these two mothers merge, that is to say, "in the coming-together in the infant's mind of the object-mother and the environment-mother."[47] At this point, the infant is acquiring a more stable inner self and can support the complex feeling of ambivalence about the one, merged mother. This is an important step on the road to care or concern which, for Winnicott is bound up with feeling useful or being of some "use." In the early stages of development it was "the opportunity to contribute that enabled concern to be within the child's capacity."[48] The opportunity to contribute generates the capacity for concern, not the other way around. Concern, then, is ultimately part of a collaboration, much as is Arendtian care, whose best expression is action in concert.

Let's take a moment, though, to note something quite striking about Winnicott's two mothers in relation to a different aspect of Arendt's account. The task of the object-mother—to see to the baby's needs, to satisfy hunger, and so on—is the domain of Arendt's Labor; and the task of the environment-mother—to provide a stable environment for the child—is the domain of Arendt's Work. Arendt's feminist commentators have long noted that Arendt's term "labor" calls to mind housework and childbirth, some noting that she herself makes the reference to female reproduction clear in her work;[49] some of those same commentators also note that with Work Arendt enters a man's world, the domain of *homo faber*, after all. Some have also called Arendt masculinist for supposedly *preferring* Work to Labor and for supposedly gendering Labor feminine and associating it, in a conventional and sexist way, with nature.[50] Winnicott's two mothers invite a reconsideration of these claims.[51]

Here we have the possibility of a different approach, one that rejects the association of Labor and Work with the proverbial Eve and Adam, the original reproductive/productive pair, and sees instead in Arendt's categories of Labor and Work Winnicott's two *mothers*, one oriented to need satisfaction and the other to the provision of a holding environment.[52] Labor and Work provide in Arendt's theory what the object- and environment-mothers respectively provide in Winnicott's: the former is tasked with satisfying our "urgent needs"; the latter with "ward[ing] off the unpredictable," as Winnicott puts it, using terms that parse perfectly well Arendt's presentation of Labor and Work. Arendt, less drawn than is Winnicott to ambivalence as a concept or affect, may be less open than he would be to the merging of Labor and Work; but her mentions of care or love for the world (*Amor Mundi*) suggest we may see some connection between her phenomenological distinctions and her desire to address the problem posed by feelings of paralysis, uselessness, or purposelessness that worry both her and Winnicott. Notably, on Winnicott's account, when these two mothers are combined, as the child develops, the sophisticated effect of the combination is not only ambivalence, the ability to experience both aggression and affection for the same single mother figure; that is just the first effect, which may end in guilt and paralysis. The second effect is the development of the capacity for concern and the ability to act on it: to offer compensation by helping the environment-mother or by making one's own contribution to the holding environment.

Arendt will call this same achievement love or care for the world. (Commentators have put particular emphasis on "care" in Arendt since Gilligan popularized that term in the 1970s.) For Arendt, such care finds expression in Action, which, to borrow Winnicott's terms for her idea, is where we act on our sense of responsibility for the world and fulfill our desire to make a contribution to it. When Arendt insists it is "still the world, and neither natural abundance nor the sheer necessity of life, which stands at the center of human care and worry,"[53] we may now hazard she is more or less in agreement with Winnicott, for whom care is what emerges once aggression regarding "sheer" needs (object-mother) and affection regarding "abundance" (environment-mother) have merged in a way that makes room for something else to happen. If we stay with the analogy with Winnicott, we may say that, for Arendt, the experience of Action presupposes the experience of both Labor and Work, and that Arendt's Work in particular creates the conditions for care which include a kind of indifference to immediate needs and a mediated relation to the world and to others. With Winnicott in the picture, it is less easy to berate Arendt for being simply and cruelly oblivious to the *needs* of the poor or disenfranchised.[54] Instead, we may see her as committed to their reification, so that they can become worldly.

As I said at the outset, my aim is not to translate Arendt into Winnicott, or vice versa. Such an operation always risks effacing key differences between the thinkers being compared and too often simply returns us to what we already knew before we began. That said, extending each one's vocabulary to rework or resituate the other's ideas has helped to highlight the distinctive contributions Arendt and Winnicott might make to a political theory of public things. Although both see objects or things as lending to us and the world a stability and permanence that are more made or achieved than found, Arendt and Winnicott differ on important details, a couple of which are especially relevant to those interested in this approach to public things. In Arendt, we have a subject seeking a durable enough object to care for, or objects durable enough to set the conditions for world care, while in Winnicott, though we may care for objects, it is the objects, specifically transitional objects, that subjectivate us into concern. Between them, then, Arendt and Winnicott set up the paradox of politics for public things in which subject and object presuppose and require each other.[55]

For Winnicott, the resilience of the object is not only factical but also fantastic; the infant's imagination is a key component of object relations. For Arendt, though, it seems like the durability of the things she writes about is merely factical. This is part of what is *attractive* about her view for those interested in defending the value of public things to democracies since, for

Arendt, their mere thingness—the fact that they outlast us—is already a contribution. Or so it seems. But this lastingness is *not* merely factical, and it is not only a trait of things as such.

Think of the table, one of Arendt's examples of a thing, favored by her readers. Commenting on it, John Kiess contrasts the table to the food served on it, in order to highlight the difference between the things of Work and the stuff of Labor. The food disappears; the table does not: "While food set upon the table is quickly consumed, the table itself has the potential to bring a family together over many meals, over many years, and potentially over many decades," he says.[56] But in marking the contrast between them, Kiess also undermines it when, incredibly, having just explained that food cannot provide the memory support that a table does, Kiess nonetheless turns to food to do just that. Hoping to illustrate Arendt's point that "remembrance and the gift of recollection" rely on "tangible things to remind them lest they perish themselves,"[57] Kiess explains: "Here Arendt is pointing to the fact that it sometimes takes an actual object—Proust's madeleine cake—to activate our memory and re-establish our connection to the past."[58] This turn to food to underwrite the table, when it is the table that is supposed to underwrite the food, is no mere contradiction. It is a key if unacknowledged recognition that the food that is supposedly, as Kiess says with Arendt, "used up in use," nonetheless lingers and contributes-in to the thingness of things. Thus, Kiess reminds us of the interdependence of table and food, how the smell, the taste, the sensations of food, lodge in us and in the table, how they help make the table what it is. The table is lasting because it *holds* the supposedly ephemeral experiences that it has hosted—the food served upon it and the gatherings held around it. Thus, the food is not only used up, it is preserved *in* the table and it preserves the table. Indeed, the table's capacity to bring us together, to hold *us*, is partly related to the fact that it holds the food we have eaten, are eating, will eat. All of this helps the table be what it is—a dining table, a family table, a homework table, or a meeting table, and not, say, an ironing board (or perhaps that, too, in which case that adds to the meaning of the table and to the breadth of its holding powers).

We know Arendt knows all this from her reading of Heine's Sabbath Poetry in her essay "The Jew as Pariah." When Heine puts the lowly Jewish Sabbath stew, which he calls Schalet, on the table of the gods alongside their nectar and ambrosia, Arendt admires the audacity of the poet's move and thus shows she knows how the meaning of the table (and that of the ancient myths!) can be altered by the food on it.[59] Heine's Jewish interruption of the Greek gods' divine eternity may be seen as an exercise of Arendtian care. As Kiess rightly points out, "the world endures not through the durability of the objects alone, but through the willingness of citizens to care for them: to repair those that have been broken [he mentions bridges and roads] and replace those that have worn out."[60] If the table of the gods has not yet worn out, it is because it has constantly been remade, reinterpreted, reset, its menus changed. Like all things, the table is made as a thing not just by way of fabrication but also in its use and reuse, in its remakings. The circularity of thingness is clear, even in Arendt's own account, *malgré elle, peut-être.* Things hold our memories and, often, their durability as things is not just independent of us but also bound up with us. Their capacity to hold us is intertwined with our holding of them. Thus, as we noted in Lecture One, the Mercier Bridge in Quebec is, for the Mohawks, and for others who pay attention, a monument to the skill and labor of early twentieth-century Native ironworkers and to the mise-en-scène (occupation and conquest) of its construction. It bridges not only space but also across time. This is how it looks, this is what it does: It holds the tribe together in memory and in futurity even while serving a similar function for Quebecois, whose public thing it also is.[61]

As we have seen, Arendt comes closest to thinking about things in such ways when she addresses fantasy. But, on Arendt's account, fantasy may explain our *mis*placed investments in things but not our capacity to invest in things in the first place, nor their ability to return the favor. Winnicott's more capacious view will be important, in Lecture Three, when we look at the role of fantasy—and dreamwork—in generating public things and at the role of public things in the democratic fantasies of collectivity that are often crucial to generating Arendtian collective power. Thing theory will go even further to call our attention to the possible agency of things beyond the circularity of their factical durability for us and the contribution of our (re)use to that durability. Things can also be noncompliant. They may reject us, failing to work in the expected ways, or recoiling upon us, their durability undone or even, and perhaps better, *manifested* by their refusal or inability to hold us and our activities.[62] In a way, this is Arendt's point about their independence from us, though she does not think of things as having agency or power. It is also her point about Parisian miniatures, though she short-circuits the question of agency's distribution when she blames the people, not the things, for making a bad investment.

Arendt's contribution to a political theory of public things is also limited by her claim that Action "goes on directly between men without the intermediary of things or matter."[63] Things may be central to the worldly capacity to occasion and remember Action, but Action itself is unmediated by objects, she insists.[64] For Winnicott, this is never so: object relations are indispensable to human relations as such and vice versa. Winnicott's insistence on the importance of things precisely to *human* relations provides a key corrective to Arendt and calls our attention to the role of things in the holding environments we build or find well past infancy. On the other hand, Arendt's perspective on Action as independent of things will call our attention to the specific experience of *public speech*, which plays a key role in the collective re-creation of the world by those who survive its destruction. (In Lecture Three, her influence will help call our attention to the role of tribal elders' speech in concert in shaping tribe members' otherwise abyssal experiences, for example.) We may say with Winnicott that speech, as such, enters onto the scene when the environment-mother, or the environment as such, fails to anticipate or address the infant's needs as quickly and perceptively as the object-mother. In the gap that opens between the environment-mother and the infant, language and symbolization enter. Speech is a way to show concern and to knit together a ruptured world. Arendt's claim that things have no role to play in (the individuating domain of) Action is, from a Winnicottian perspective, an overstated way of making this point.

Winnicott's holding environment, a site of care, handling, and holding, is instructive for us, since we may think about public things as constituting a kind of *democratic holding environment*, a laboratory for citizenship in which we experience lifelong the attachments and play that form and re-form all of us into individuated and resilient persons, capable of aggression, concern, and the self-collection they postulate.[65] Winnicott may not have had in mind the public parks, libraries, and bridges I focus on here, but what he does say about object relations can be extended in this direction if we think of the interpellative powers of the public things that fold subjects into citizenship as properties of transitional objects.[66] This is where Winnicott's focus on magic and fantasy can take us.

To analyze the workings of transitional objects in the holding environment, Winnicott says we should attend to:

1. The nature of the object.
2. The infant's capacity to recognize the object as "not-me."
3. The place of the object—outside, inside, at the border.
4. The infant's capacity to create, think up, devise, originate, produce an object [that is to say, the infant's imagination, creativity, spontaneity].
5. The initiation of an affectionate type of object-relationship [which could include rage, as well as love].[67]

Not me and yet in a relationship with or to me (ours?), devised by us, positioned between us, loved by us, or hated, and available for communal play, these are among the traits that describe a democratic orientation to public things, those things over which we lack sovereign mastery but which are nonetheless inescapably ours or us and which constitute what Arendt and Winnicott both call the "between" that binds and individuates us. "The interplay between separateness and union" has many instances, on Winnicott's account. One is the "interplay between originality and the acceptance of tradition as the basis for inventiveness."[68] We may think of this as the practice of relating to public things in ways that express, extend, and maybe even test our deepest commitments. This formulation is consistent with Arendt's account, elsewhere, of authority, a concept she aligns with "augmentation" to suggest that the recognition of authority consists not in obedience or conformity but rather in inventive and innovative practices, connected to their precedents but not duplicative of them.[69] This is like the "use" which *adds* to the thingness of things and does not only deplete them.

Drawing on Winnicott, we might think of neoliberalism's incessant demand for privatization in connection with object relations' raging child. Both act in ways that undermine the object in relation to which they operate. The blanket may be torn or dirtied by the emotional child and loved all the more as a result. But the public goods that are increasingly privatized may be irretrievably lost by the antipathy to and dismantling of the public thing, as such, in favor of private funding, hybrid models, ever lower taxation. We learn from Winnicott that the loving-destructive child is engaged in a kind of reality testing. Aiming to destroy the object, the child craves its survival.

When it witnesses the object's survival, the child finds comfort and nurturance; the resilient object teaches him or her the limits of his or her own powers and in so doing s/he acquires new capacities, including the capacity for concern which is, as Winnicott says, "at the back of all constructive play and work."[70]

Perhaps neoliberalization is its own kind of reality testing: acting out the urge to destroy public things, while needing them to survive so as to learn limitation and finitude. In Winnicott, it is key that the object resists and survives the infant's emotional drama. Only in this way can the infant move past its grandiose omnipotence and dependency on the object, into play with it and beyond it (poetry, culture, politics). Politically, of course, the survival of the public thing—climate, the planet, health care—cannot be taken for granted and so the reality that is tested may yield to the test rather than the other way round. Perhaps this is why world-endingness is such a common trope in contemporary theory and film: not just because we need to work through our finitude as we face the proverbial end, but because the theories and films, terrifying as they are, paradoxically constitute a holding environment. They do not just warn about the loss of public things; they take their place and offer an opportunity for guilt and rage to develop into the kinds of ambivalence and concern that public things presuppose and require.

The Arendtian/Winnicottian vernacular of care and concern developed here will help us explore these questions in *Radical Hope*, Jonathan Lear's book on loss, catastrophe, and the redemptiveness of land, and in *Melancholia*, Lars von Trier's film on those same themes. As we shall see, public things play a key, if unthematized, role in both. What Lear calls "radical hope" is the maintenance of the capacity for concern absent nearly all its necessary conditions. What Lars von Trier will offer is a depiction of the singular capacity of a natal child to conjure the environment-mother when she has gone missing, to then merge the object- and environment-mothers and, like the hero of Lear's book, to secure hope and act out of concern for the world even when it seems all is lost. In von Trier, in particular, fantasy is a crucial part of hope's resilience in the face of utter, utter catastrophe. Hope is not enough of course; but it is something. And it is not all we have, for, as we learn from both Winnicott and Arendt, things often exceed our power to destroy or preserve them. And so it turns out that long after we have forgotten them, they are still there, like the public phones after Hurricane Sandy, still possessed of the power to feed our imaginations of possible futures, help pull us through the paradox of politics when we face it anew, and provide the mirroring unity that might stimulate creative new projects of self-organization and self-collection in democratic settings.

Hope and Play: Jonathan Lear's *Radical Hope and* Lars von Trier's *Melancholia*

I turn now from the question of care and concern in the (democratic) hold-ing environment to ask: What might hope, as represented by Jonathan Lear's *Radical Hope*, and play, as represented by Lars von Trier's *Melancholia*, have to offer a Winnicottian/Arendtian analysis of the necessary conditions of democratic life?

As we saw in Lecture Two, holding environments offer the handling and holding that facilitate our attachment to transitional objects whose unity models a unity we have yet to achieve. Transitional objects survive our de-structive passions and moods, help us develop a capacity for concern, and occasion our care for and contributions to others and the world. These are elements of child development on D. W. Winnicott's account, and they map well onto Arendt's account of Work, the domain in which we create things that survive intact our neglect, if not our full-on destructiveness. Arendt does not comment on the psychic aspects of Work. But when she positions Work between Labor and Action, attributes to Work the capacity to interrupt the process-like character of Labor and Work, says that Works provides the stability that neither Labor nor Work can secure, and informs us that the manmade things of Work demand ordinary care and maintenance from us, everything she says seems to describe a "holding environment," and her account comes awfully close to Winnicott's.

What I have added to Arendt's and Winnicott's accounts is some alertness, courtesy of contemporary thing theory, to the recalcitrance of some objects, their resistance to our purposes/interpretations or to any purposes/ interpretations. We may get this sort of insight about the recalcitrance of objects, albeit without attributing agency to them, also even from Winnicott and Arendt, though. In both these thinkers' work, we find some awareness that things can betray the psychic and Work investments we make in them. Some things may *not* survive, in fantasy, our destruction of them. They may let us down. Winnicott knows this. Arendt does, too. She notes that some things, rather than stabilize our world and create sites of adhesion and attachment to it, may become vehicles of world alienation. One of her examples is Galileo's telescope, which, by showing that the earth was not at the center of all planet life, undid the teleologies that organized human living and Christian faith, inviting detachment from the world. The telescope plays a key role in Lars von Trier's film *Melancholia*, where it also provides a new, anti-teleological angle on things. Von Trier's film features not only a real telescope but also a child's toy telescope, an irony, surely, in that it is the child's plaything (not the real telescope) that provides the perspective from which our earth is revealed to be the mere plaything of another planet.[1]

I turn now to look at von Trier's film together with Jonathan Lear's book *Radical Hope*. Both explore the loss of holding environments and the worldloss that results. Both pose the question of how and whether attachment to world and to others is possible in such contexts, in particular in the absence of public things. And both offer, wittingly or otherwise, alternative holdings to which we may resort when deprived of the public things needed for democratic life. Arendt does the same, as we saw in Lecture One, when she writes about life after catastrophe.[2] She knows that people who are deprived of worldly things that situate them among others are forced to find inner resources for moral and political orientation, and that not all succeed. Most do not. But when she talks about political action in *The Human Condition*, insisting that action occurs between men without the intermediary of things or matter, she seems to suggest action without public things is possible— and even desirable. In Lecture Two, I suggested, *contra* Arendt, that surely things are at work even among actors in concert, but I noted that her insistence to the contrary is useful, for it calls us to attend specifically to the unique speech characteristic of this one domain, and to the possible capacity of such speech on its own to meet the needs of the holding environment when nothing else can do so. When Arendt goes on, later in *The Human Condition*, to specify promising and forgiveness as exemplary in the domain of Action, she lights on the capacity of *speech* to provide the handling and holding (forgiving and promising) provided by Winnicott's good enough mother in the holding environment. Promising elicits from the self the unity (in time and space) it seeks to achieve.[3] Forgiveness paradoxically underwrites that unity by relaxing it just enough so we can go on.

For the sake of democracies deprived of public things, it may be important to learn what we can from Arendt, here. As we shall see, Lear's account of the speech of tribal elders to young men of the tribe features these traits of promising and forgiveness: the elders fold the young men's stories into larger tribal narratives that hold their uncontainable emotions (fear and guilt). And in von Trier's film, an adult who still knows how to play is able to help when called upon to do so: she creates a holding environment for a youth whose world-ending fear of maturation—or whose desire for world-ending change—might be the end of him.

These themes of maturation, transition, and holding were brought together in the U.S. election season of 2012, when Republican presidential candidate Mitt Romney opened the first presidential debate by promising to cut government funding to PBS. He linked public things quite powerfully to transitional objects when he used Sesame Street's Big Bird as a metaphor for the public network: "I like PBS. I love Big Bird. Actually, I like you too," Romney said to the debate moderator Jim Lehrer, who for decades had hosted PBS's *NewsHour*.[4] "But I'm not going to keep on spending money on things to borrow money from China to pay for."[5] After the debate, progressives aired TV ads defending Big Bird, showing the large yellow creature standing in Depression-era soup kitchen lines or holding a sign that said "will work for food."[6]

By using Big Bird as a figure for public things, Romney cast public things like PBS as childish, as an early form of dependence that we, as a democracy, are supposed to outgrow and eventually leave behind.[7] This is the language in which social welfare programs are also wrapped by critics on the Right, as infantilizing sources of dependence from which the poor need to be weaned, like babies from the breast. Increasingly, such arguments have broadened in recent years to include public things as such, and citizens in general, not just social services and not just the poor. Countering that narration now requires thinking about other ways to depict democratic maturation; it will require counternarrations of the democratic need for public things, in which such needs are cast not as infantile, but as mature, or simply human.

First, though, there are some points to be made by way of critique: the same people who call for us to be weaned off of public programs and public things often also seek out government subsidies for the classes or interests they support as independent and mature: farmers in some quarters (though really it is more often agribusiness), banks in others. These subsidized parties are never cast as childlike.[8] But pointing out hypocrisy or contradiction is not enough. We are too used to exposé, and besides, when we unmask the falseness of the autonomy claimed by others, we buy into the standard of autonomy that casts dependency as infantile and autonomy as maturity. This standard, associated with particular philosophical and political economies, marginalizes other democratic civic ideals, which might include interdependence and a shared need for public things around which to constellate, gather, and differ.

"Everybody loves Big Bird!" was the refrain after that first 2012 presidential debate. This is not just funny, though it is that, too. If everyone loves Big Bird that may well be because Big Bird meets the democratic need. The beloved character may *represent* democracy's rootedness in common love for shared objects, or even in contestation of them, for such contestation betrays a common love, more than sentimental claims of devotion do.[9] Connecting past and future, the transitional object that teaches concern may also teach "hope."

Recall here the line from the Emily Dickinson poem, in which hope is described as "the thing with feathers. . . ."[10]

"Hope" is the thing with feathers—
That perches in the soul—
And sings the tune without the words—
And never stops—at all—
And sweetest—in the Gale—is heard—
And sore must be the storm—
That could abash the little Bird
That kept so many warm—
I've heard it in the chillest land—
And on the strangest Sea—
Yet—never—in Extremity,
It asked a crumb—of me

The 1891 poem predates Big Bird, the big yellow "thing with feathers"; but maybe Big Bird's creators knew their Dickinson?

Often, the response of political or social theorists to the loss of public things is to lament their passing while insisting on their enduring value or, sometimes, to renounce them totally in embrace of the new. Lear and von Trier look at the failure of public things and public rituals to do their psycho-symbolic work of enchantment and meaning-making, and both identify the resources that remain and on which we must draw for the sake of a possible future. In von Trier's film, rituals fail to work because their time and tempo have been absorbed by the time and temporality of neoliberal *work*. As work rises into a full-time occupation, absorbing the time and worth of other practices and pastimes, some of the protagonists are tempted by melancholy and suicide. In Lear's book, too, old rituals for dealing with rupture or loss no longer work, and people must figure out how to deal with the loss of loss, as it were, and—I might add—how to respond politically to the loss of public things. The destructive forces are settler colonialism, capitalism (and maybe liberalism but not *neo*liberalism), and white supremacy. Some Native people seek out messianism while some yield to despair, Lear says, noting that melancholy and suicidal behavior are key temptations.

But others reach for realism.[11] In *Radical Hope*, Lear promotes what he calls realism or realistic action by contrasting it with the inaction to which, he says, messianism and despair invariably lead.[12] One of his examples of such doomed messianism is the Ghost Dance, in which, as we shall see below, Sitting Bull, the Sioux chief, placed a great deal of faith. The Dance was a potentially transformative, public ritual, and in sidelining it, Lear focuses on "hope" to the exclusion of "play"; arguably von Trier's film does the opposite.

So Lear's framework is problematic, and my aim is not to endorse it as such. But it is useful to a political theory of public things to note that one of the key elements of the realism Lear lauds involves the renewal of public things. Lear's book *Radical Hope* asks what allowed the Crow people to pass through a catastrophic destruction of their world and, somehow, come out the other side with some semblance of a future.[13] The Crow people, aboriginal to the United States, stood on the brink of destruction in the mid–nineteenth century, facing white supremacy, an environment deprived of its capacity to sustain their way of life, and a violent politics of settler conquest. Recounting the story of the Crow, Lear develops an account of the repertoires of resilience drawn upon by this people threatened with extinction, and on which others might draw now and in the future. The result is an account that, notwithstanding its focus on catastrophe (or, as Lear calls it, "cultural devastation"), tries to ritualize rather than catastrophize radical change, which is a useful counter to the catastrophizing tendency of a great deal of contemporary Left theory. Central to Lear are hope (not mere optimism), and resilience. He does not use that second term, but he is seeking something like it, something more than mere survival in the context of catastrophe. He sometimes calls it courage.

The hero of Lear's story is the perspicuous and pragmatic Crow Chief, Plenty Coups, who leads his people through the end of life as they know it and out the other side. More Starbuck than Ahab, Plenty Coups grew up among the free Crow around the time that Melville was writing *Moby-Dick* (1850), soon after Tocqueville wrote *Democracy in America* (1830s). We know about Plenty Coups in detail because he told his life story to a white man, Sign-Talker, who lived nearby, and he wrote it down. It is on this account that Lear tenderly draws in *Radical Hope*.

Lear notes the melancholic note in Plenty Coups' narrative when, after recounting his happy youth, he says that then the buffalo went away (in fact, they were diverted as a settler strategy of conquest), and "after this, nothing happened."[14] Lear's book is a rumination on this statement: what can it mean, "nothing happened"?[15] Lear considers but rejects the idea that Plenty Coups was melancholic. He concedes that "some depressed people can keep

busy—as a way of warding off depression" but insists that Plenty Coups seems
to have been enthusiastically busy.[16] His life was full. He took up farming,
won prizes for his produce, united the Crow chiefs to renegotiate their treaties with the United States, and traveled to Washington to defend Crow
rights. Plenty Coups also encouraged Crow youth to get a "white" education.
He visited Mount Vernon, was impressed by the public thingness of the
home of George Washington, and decided to donate his own home as a
national park, a plan that encountered some difficulties but eventually
culminated in Chief Plenty Coups State Park. He represented American
Indians at the Tomb of the Unknown Soldier in the wake of World War I.
Such life-making after catastrophe is quite different from the keeping-busy
or the doing-nothing associated with depression, Lear protests.[17] It certainly
looks like Plenty Coups exhibited what Winnicott calls "concern."

Still, Lear admits that we cannot rule out rival interpretations: "the historical evidence is compatible with" many other interpretations. Besides the
realism, pragmatism, ritualization, and healthy adjustment that Lear sees,
we could see in Plenty Coups evidence of depression, melancholy, alienation,
submission, defeat, complicity, self-betrayal, and more.[18] One possible interpretation of the materials Lear presents could surely be that Plenty Coups,
in adjusting to the needs of the moment and accommodating himself to white
supremacy, lived a life of what D. W. Winnicott would call social conformism,[19] or what Hannah Arendt called a *parvenu* life, the sort of inauthentic
life pressed on pariahs everywhere by coercive majorities or governments
and frozen into place by the sheer unimaginability in those contexts of what
Arendt took to be the only decent alternative in such contexts—that of the
"conscious pariah."[20] Alternatively, Plenty Coups' seeming hyperactivity
could suggest a sense of guilt or remorse, since Plenty Coups led his tribe
into an alliance with whites against rival tribes like the Sioux.[21] In so doing,
the Crow unwittingly helped bring about their own near destruction. Once
the area was pacified with their help, more whites moved to settle there and,
in a series of renegotiated treaties, the U.S. government appropriated ever
more Crow land.

But Lear presses forward with his picture of Plenty Coups. On Lear's
account, the Crow chief is richly imaginative and resilient, with a gift for
ritualization. The Crow leader shepherded his people through a catastrophe,
which—because of his vision and talents—they did more than *survive.* They

also managed to retain some of their ancestral land and were therefore left with a possible, if unknowable, future. All this is owed, on Lear's account, to Plenty Coups and his great ability to lead his people into the unknown without succumbing to the temptations of either messianism or despair.

Lear concedes that the Crow strategy of allying with whites against other tribes, in order to preserve their own lands, might be called collaboration. "In the face of an onslaught by a dominant civilization, Plenty Coups decided to collaborate with it."[22] But, Lear argues, courage rather than collaboration is the important term here. For us to see this, we need to see that the very meaning of courage, in a time of radical transformation, had to undergo some change: "in particular," says Lear, "there had to be a *thinning* out of what had been a thick concept."[23]

Crow courage once involved a communal life of intertribal warfare, horse stealing, and buffalo hunting. But under white occupation, these were criminalized. Consequently, Crow courage had to be resignified, redirected; it had to give way to a more thinned-out concept, unembedded in a way of life now lost yet not so unmoored as to be meaningless, merely utopian, or reckless, and not reducible to some sort of collaboration. The mechanism for the switch from thick to thin courage is Lear's "radical hope," which enables transition. Indeed, we could analogize it to D. W. Winnicott's "transitional object"—the blanket, the stuffed animal, or the Big Bird that enables a child to manage the trauma of transition—and we might perhaps even think of radical hope as a *transitional affect*. On Lear's account, this is what the Crow clung to as they moved from one form of life to another through an abyss.

Like Winnicott's transitional object, radical hope, on Lear's account, provides the world with the permanence it lacks.[24] Radical hope takes the place of the object, since the transition in question is forced on us by the fact that the object has gone missing. Where for Winnicott, such transitions require a "holding environment" which is the performative product and postulate of transitional activity (e.g., being held and handled, handholding, play),[25] radical hope is Lear's response to the unavailability of such environments. It is his name for what gets us through traumatic transitions without the objects and environments that Winnicott thought were central to healthy transitions.[26]

Thus, radical hope is a key element in any repertoire of resilience. But, though Lear does not note it in detail, so is the capacity to judge when not

to transition, when to resist, when to fight back. Such efforts might also require radical hope and Lear acknowledges this when he says that even if less
charitable readings of Plenty Coups are right, even if his responses to White
domination were self-serving, misguided, or collaborationist, these would
also still postulate radical hope. What is centrally important to Lear is that
Plenty Coups did not give in to messianism or despair. In sum, radical hope
is what allows the Crow to go on in some "Crow" way even after the ways
of the Crow have been destroyed and their public things are gone: there are
no more buffalo to hunt, no rival tribes to fight, no room to roam, no coups
to count. Without all this, Crow life and Crow virtues seem to be unsustainable. But, Lear says at the end of his book, "a case can be made that Plenty
Coups offered the Crow a *traditional* way of going forward."[27] The hope that
drove Plenty Coups "was a remarkable human accomplishment—in no
small part because it avoided despair."[28]

"This is a daunting form of commitment to a goodness in the world that
transcends one's current ability to grasp what it is," says Lear, in keeping
with Hannah Arendt's idea of care for the world.[29] For Lear, Plenty Coups
had that commitment and the vision engendered by it. He saw within au-
thentic Crow values a thinned-out alternative that was pliable enough and
functional enough to manage in the context of a new world order of land
ownership, private property, U.S. federal governance, and white man's education, a world bereft of the old Crow things, rituals, and relations. Lear
sees in Plenty Coups a transformational, honorable leader who models neither capitulation nor collaboration, but rather a flexible realism that can be
rightly called courageous and provides a welcome counter to our contemporary tendency to romanticize martyrs as moral heroes (here Lear is
thinking of Sitting Bull) and dismiss pragmatists as unprincipled. Plenty
Coups saved his people by imagining a future, unknowable and elusive,
and building it.

In his repertoire was also the capacity to "dream" a way forward. As a
youth, alone in the woods for a few days as part of a tribal ritual of manhood,
Plenty Coups dreamed of a storm that would fell all but one of the trees of
the forest. On that one, lone surviving tree was a chickadee, a humble member of the Crow people's aviary pantheon, noted for its capacity to listen
and adaptively change course.[30] When Plenty Coups returned, he told the

dream to the tribal elders who interpreted it to mean that the Crow would face some catastrophe (white conquest, represented by the dream's devastating storm) and that to survive it they would have to adapt from Crow virtues to Chickadee ones, trading one sort of courage (martial) for another (adaptation, innovation) in a move from war virtues to more humble habits like listening, observing, and adapting to new situations. The elders thought that the Chickadee, who was no Crow, would have to be repurposed as a new icon of a new kind of courage and take the old Crow's place.[31] As one tribal elder put it: "The tribes who have *fought* the White man have all been beaten, wiped out. By listening as the Chickadee listens, we may escape this and keep our lands."[32]

But what would it *mean* to keep or hold land? It *had* meant the "ability to roam freely, in nomadic fashion, in what, from the white man's perspective, was a large but vaguely defined space around the Little Big Horn." But it would come to mean something very different: confinement to two million acres, forced to parcel property out to individual owners rather than hold lands collectively, with some of these sold off to white farmers, and so on. In short, what it *meant* to hold land would change radically,[33] and in ways that would surely alter the land's capacity to serve as a holding environment for the tribe. To hold land once meant to be held by it.

It is important, Lear argues, that the transition to the Chickadee made sense to the Crow. It did not come out of nowhere. The Crow knew themselves as the Absarokee, which means "children of the large-beaked bird." French trappers and traders (perhaps mistakenly) took that bird to be a crow, hence the tribe's English name. In the switch from Crow to Chickadee, we see an adjustment to a different admired bird, but we could also see a diminution. We go from a big bird to a small one. There is no ambivalence in Lear's celebration of this diminution.[34] For him, the chickadee is the tribe's transitional object, in effect. It secures for the Crow something more than mere survival (the chickadee is an honored bird among the Crow) and something less than suicidal martyrdom. To insist on Crow life, as it was before, in the face of white supremacy, meant certain death, says Lear, who never asks whether things *might* have turned out differently had the Crow entered into a pan-Indian alliance against whites, as the Sioux chief Sitting Bull wanted them to do. (Lear assumes the inevitability of white conquest and in so doing buys in, in a way, to the tribal elders' reading of the storm imagery of Plenty Coup's boyhood dream/vision—the disaster is inevitable and possessed of natural force.)[35]

Recall how, in *The Human Condition*, Hannah Arendt mocks the Parisians for their love of small things.[36] This she saw as mere attachment to fetish, a symptom of their lost glory, a painful sign of their withdrawal from the once glorious days of Empire and public worldliness. Lear, by contrast, tries to find something to value precisely in attachment to small(er) things, in part because he sees the attachment in question as transitional and not fetishistic. The move from Crow to Chickadee is, for Lear, a continuation of Crow life and it lays the groundwork for an eventual rebirth. Lear goes to great lengths to find in the post catastrophic period of native genocide, from World War I to the almost present-day, examples of Crow rebirth and resurrection. The Crow restart their lost ritual of the Sun Dance, Lear points out, though he concedes that in order to do so they must learn the steps of a different dance from a rival tribe, once an enemy. No Crow can recall the steps of the tribe's own dance. It is lost to time.

Lear does not put it this way, but it is important, I think, that Plenty Coups was sensitive to his tribe's need for an infrastructure of public things to support their new life. Plenty Coups understood the importance of public things and some of his were larger than life. He did not allow everything to be diminished. In 1919, after the war, representing not the Crow but the Indians of the United States—the very pan-Indian identity to which Sitting Bull tried unsuccessfully to recruit him a world ago—Plenty Coups presented a Native war headdress and other Native martial objects at the Tomb of the Unknown Soldier, the U.S. memorial to the war dead.[37] The objects were laid at the memorial. Lear argues that this should be seen as ritual burial: Plenty Coups symbolically buries the tokens of a former way of life.[38] Lear approves of this ritualization of the loss. It "clear[s] the ground for a rebirth . . . for if the death is not acknowledged there will likely be all sorts of empty ways of going on 'as a Crow.'" Lear worries, however, that the rebirth might be just "nostalgia or ersatz mimesis." What is needed is a new Crow poet, he says, in "the broadest sense of a creative maker of meaningful space." For Lear, Plenty Coups is that poet, a dream poet. Plenty Coups' poetry is his story: he told his story "in order to preserve it," Lear says, "and he did so in the hope of a future in which things—Crow things—might start to happen again."[39] Here, I think, Lear is on to something. It is Plenty Coup's gift to ritualize but also, and more specifically, to *refurnish* the world. He sees the importance of refilling his people's emptied world with things that matter, public things, around which to constellate, to which to attach, over which to fight.

As Lear sees him, Plenty Coups dreams a way through his tribe's anxiety about illness, tribal conflict, and white conquest and plots a realist, pragmatic solution to an intractable problem: how to move through catastrophe with some measure of authenticity (in a Crow way) toward a future that cannot be known, in which the values and skills of the quickly passing present will be useless and valueless, but in which his people might reattach, nonetheless, to the Crow world of Crow ritual. Plenty Coups' "courageous actions" both enable a relatively favorable political outcome (the Crow negotiate to settle in present-day Montana, their ancestral land) and help the tribe maintain "the psychological resources" to face the "loss of concepts," survive, and maybe even go on to thrive.[40] What we may add to Lear is that Plenty Coups understood that success in all this depended on the tribe's capacity to refurnish its world with public things. Hence his many efforts to provide his tribe with such things.

There are three others whom Lear takes to serve as contrasts to Plenty Coups' admirable example. Pretty Shield is a Crow medicine woman who simply goes on with her various duties (such as cooking) from before the break, but these are unmoored to the public or ritual purposes that once made them make sense (cooking for Crow fighters before battle). It is as if she, who was once an environment-mother, can now serve only as object-mother. Cooking without purpose, she says she is "trying to live a life I do not understand."[41] From this attachment to the past and placelessness in the present, Lear intimates, no future can come. James Martel suggests otherwise, however, noting that in Lear's own depiction of Pretty Shield, we see that "the food remains and is always available for a reestablishment of rituals." Martel is right. As we saw in the Introduction and Lecture One, in Guatemala the Mayans say that corn instructs them in how to live their lives in resistance to Monsanto imperatives. The food speaks, as it were. Indigenous food and the natural infrastructure also provide native peoples in British Columbia the bases of indigenous action in concert in protection of a way of life threatened by new pipelines. Cooking, once an emptied ritual, is reborn as political practice. Recall what we saw in Lecture Two, how the Arendtian table's meaning as a stable object derives precisely from the food served on it, even though Arendt would say that food, by contrast with a table, is not possessed of object permanence at all. When Pretty Shield cooks and laments the lack of meaning in her practice, she is nonetheless in an object-relation and the object may surprise her. The food carries meanings and promises beyond what can be apprehended in one (desolate) moment. The food may be a thinned out shadow of its former self, as it were, or it may signpost an enriching future. It may starve or feed us and there is no way of knowing which it will be since that depends, in part, on how we relate to it as an object now and in the future. Do we take up its invitation?

Then there is Sitting Bull, the great Sioux chief who is taken in, Lear says (as we saw earlier), by the "false" messianic promise of the Ghost Dance. For Lear, Sitting Bull lacks the realism to face his people's true circumstances, which demand radical, not messianic hope.[42] But as Jason Frank argues, Sitting Bull was hardly inactive or removed from the realities of the dire situation facing his people. He hoped his visions and the Ghost Dance "would usher in an apocalyptic punishing of the whites and a restoration of the Sioux to their previous way of life. Lear casts this as 'little more than a dangerous fantasy,'" but, Frank rightly replies, "It is worth remembering that Sitting Bull's Ghost Dance so worried U.S. authorities for its subversive potential that they actively tried to suppress it, and that Sitting Bull also attempted to organize a pan-Indian alliance. . . . Who is to say whether such a strategy—when viewed from the perspective of the actors confronting the catastrophic political situation before them, rather than looking back on events from over a century of subsequent history—indicated a state of denial or acting out on the basis of a 'false messianic promise?'"[43] Sitting Bull's efforts to build a pan-Indian alliance are dismissed by Lear as lacking the realism called for in this dire situation, though such action in concert might have had real effects.

Finally, there is Wraps His Tail, a young male Crow, who goes on acting as if the old ways were still viable. He leads a horse raid (forbidden by whites) to retaliate against a rival tribe, and when he returns to celebrate, he confusedly finds he is charged with a crime rather than honored as a tribal hero. Under arrest, he is shot by another Crow working for the settler police.[44]

Lear does not countenance Wraps His Tail's actions as anything but defeatist. But there is resistance here: Wraps His Tail refuses the diminution that Plenty Coups pragmatically accepts. Again, the historical outcome overly drives Lear's reading, surely. James Martel notes "Lear's hostility both to Sitting Bull's support for the Ghost Dance movement and even Wraps His Tails' insistence on continuing to live according to the old Crow ways. These," Martel argues, "are seen [by Lear] as romantic or messianic gestures when in fact they represent a political and creative response to a terrible (but not hopeless) situation."[45]

Dismissing the other three types, Lear clears the way for Plenty Coups who, on Lear's account, transforms catastrophe into a "political" situation to be managed. Few people who have seen the film would consider von Trier's *Melancholia* as doing the same thing, but I think there is a case to be made for that by looking at the film's transformation of despair into play. Like Lear, Von Trier explores some repertoires of resilience and underlines the importance of ritual in dealing with rupture and, like Lear, von Trier explores how to respond to catastrophe. But surely von Trier, unlike Lear's Plenty Coups, catastrophizes a situation—climate change, planetary survival—that is arguably not best seen in apocalyptic terms? Climate change is an issue that radical democratic actors should seek not only to survive or manage but also to shape. In von Trier's favor, however, we may say that he is not analogizing: he may offer a parable, rather, to mobilize those who might otherwise succumb to what they simply assume, wrongly and dangerously, to be inevitable.[46] Witnessing inevitable destruction, we may be moved out of passivity and into action. We may say the same about Lear. In my view, his book and von Trier's film may be seen as two parables of democracy in disrepair.

In Lars von Trier's *Melancholia*, there are *two* calamities in play. A rogue planet named Melancholia may be about to collide with the earth in a kind of suicide collision that will destroy them both. For those who focus on this first calamity in von Trier's film, Justine, the main character, who herself suffers from melancholia, is a way for von Trier (who also suffers from melancholia) to explore a "truth" reportedly once imparted to the director by a therapist: that melancholics are good at handling catastrophe, because they are more prepared for it than are other people. The film's second calamity is that of neoliberal life itself, in which work is ceaseless, the time and tempo of work expand to take in everything, wealth provides its own warped table of values, and rituals that once promised to give meaning to life do not "work."

The second calamity is illustrated most forcefully by the presence at Justine's wedding of her boss, an advertising executive, who is there as a guest but who has brought along an underling for the express purpose of getting one last tag line from Justine before she goes away on her honeymoon. The underling hovers, hopefully (and gets more than he bargained for), while the boss accosts her repeatedly, hoping to profit from her creativity. In this way and others, the film mocks the neoliberal assumption of the 24/7 workday, even enjoying its clichéd politics of refusal when Justine finally tells her boss what she really thinks of him, and he leaves in a fit of pique. (Justine: "Nothing is too much for you, Jack. I hate you and your firm so deeply I couldn't find the words to describe it. You are a despicable power-hungry little man, Jack." Jack: "Is that a resignation? Because they aren't too many jobs out there, I tell you."[47]) There are other neoliberal indicators as well: Justine's brother-in-law, John, owns an estate with a golf course, the site of the wedding party, and keeps referring to how much money he has spent on her wedding, willing her to be happy in return as if money could buy happiness. The ill-fatedness of the wedding is a sign of the incapacity of old rituals to meet the demands of the moment (though, more accurately, they have never fully met the demand of any moment). Whatever their past successes and failures, they surely cannot work in the new political-economic context.

Thus, rather than see the film as an effort to depict the special preparedness of melancholics for catastrophe, we may see it as an effort to show how the catastrophe of neoliberalism makes, or ought to make, melancholics of us all. On this reading, we could say (in Benjamin's wake) the crash of planets has already happened and we just do not know it yet. Like some melancholics, we are all just going through the motions of everyday life, some of us not at all attuned to the devastation that surrounds us, many of us living in it, a few of us resisting it and pointing it out. As these lines will already indicate, we are not far from Lear's terrain here. Indeed, all four types explored by Lear have their parallels in the von Trier film. First, there is John, who demands happiness from the melancholic Justine (as if she could will it) and later commits suicide when faced with catastrophe. Since he refuses to look real reality full in the face, putting his faith in the false promise of the scientists who say the collision will not occur, John recalls Lear's version of Sitting Bull, whom Lear casts as reality-avoidant. (The other Sitting Bull, invoked by Martel, Frank, and myself, the one who actively sought political and military responses to devastating events, is not represented in von Trier.) With his suicide, John actually does the neoliberal thing: He *opts out*, and like all opt-outs, he does so at some cost to others. He commits suicide with a bottle of sleeping pills that his wife, Claire, had bought for herself and their son, Leo, to use in the event of catastrophe. Now she will not be able to sleep through the end.

Second, there is Claire, Justine's sister, who plays the role of Pretty Shield, the Crow woman who goes on cooking and says she is living a life she does not understand. Claire wants to greet the end of the world with a soiree. She asks Justine to meet her for a glass of wine on the terrace. "I want us to be together when it happens. . . . Help me. Justine. I want it to be nice. . . . We could have a glass of wine. . . . What do you say, Sis?" Justine responds: "Do you want to hear what I think of your plan? I think it's a piece of shit! You want it to be nice? Why don't we do it in the fuckin' toilet?" (This is Justine's nonconformism.) Claire seems unable to innovate for the new event, which she cannot comprehend.[48] Pretty Shield also cannot innovate, she goes on cooking after cultural obliteration, but at least she is also able to say, "I am trying to live a life I do not understand." In so saying, she holds the place for a possible return one day to cooking with meaning. From "I am trying to live a life I do not understand" it is not *that* far to "I demand that the life I live be one I can understand."

Third, there is the young boy, Claire's son, Leo. Leo is like Lear's Wraps His Tail. In their last hours or minutes, both youths play in the natural state until their young male play is aborted by the impact of seemingly unavoidable events. Wraps His Tail's play is political because it has been outlawed. Leo's play is political in a different way; faced with the destruction of a life he cannot bear, the looming catastrophe becomes a stage for something new. Leo either has or dreams something Wraps His Tail did not: a visionary aunt, a mother-figure whom he enlists in play and who establishes a holding environment for or with her nephew.

That aunt, Justine, represents the fourth way forward or into the abyss. In the face of disaster, Justine insists on authenticity and seems to blossom only when she is outside, often in commune with animals or acting like them. Of the four types on offer from Lear, she is most like Plenty Coups in these

ways and more (though she is more principled than pragmatic). She innovates for the moment and creates a playful game, enlisting her young nephew
in the project of building what she calls "a magic cave." When Justine and
the boy play together, she heeds Winnicott's admonition to the philosopher
to "*come out of his chair and sit on the floor with his patient.*"[49] She and her nephew
cut and carve wood together and he works with increasing independence with
the knife needed for the task. For the first time in a long while, it seems,
things "are happening" at the estate. Justine rejects Claire's proposed social
ritual (wine on the terrace does not address Leo's needs, nor Justine's) and
makes up a new one that is more responsive to events and more attuned to
human needs. Rather than self-anesthetize or go through the motions of once
joyous rituals, Justine, like Plenty Coups, innovates by drawing on an existing repertoire (building treehouses, playing pretend) to create a new ritual—
building a magic cave—even as catastrophe looms. Lear might see this play
as a thinning out of prior practices but we could just as well see it as a thickening that makes things happen. In any case, like Plenty Coups, Justine is
helping to furnish an empty world.

Birds have a role to play here as well, and so do signs, portent, omens,
and prophecy. Again, like Plenty Coups who sees things, Justine "know[s]
things." She, too, has a vision of the future in which catastrophe comes but,
rather than one lone surviving chickadee in a tree, she sees birds falling like
dead weights from the sky. Instead of the Chickadee of the Crow's aviary
pantheon, we have here something more like Chicken Little, but this time
the sky really *is* falling. There are no tribal elders to interpret the vision and
so Justine is isolated by her visions, and they are never integrated into her
tribe's reality at all.

Justine's magic cave won't "work," not if surviving catastrophic collision
is the aim. And, as we saw earlier, it is hard to say whether Plenty Coups'
innovations "worked," either, in that same sense. Are the Crow still Crow,
once they are living on the reservation and oriented to Chickadee ways? Lear
stipulates that they are, approving the elasticity of their aviary pantheon and
setting aside concerns about whether we can rightly call this sort of altera-
tion an adaptation or even think of it as *survival*.[50] With von Trier's help,
we gain a new perspective on Plenty Coups because in Justine's ritual the
aim is clearly not survival. Her aim, and perhaps this should be the measure
of Plenty Coups as well (and of Sitting Bull!), is to face reality in a way that

has some redemptive honesty or authenticity.[51] The magic cave is not falsely hopeful. This is Lear's charge against Sitting Bull's relation to the Ghost Dance. Justine, Claire, and maybe even Leo all know these twigs and branches will not protect them from world destruction. Yet, at the same time, building the magic cave is not just a *going through the motions* either. Like the Ghost Dance, this play may itself be something of a revolutionary act.

The cave serves another purpose, just as the Ghost Dance, dismissed as unrealistic by Lear, may have served another purpose as well, in a way that Lear does not consider. The cave and the process of building it give the boy—and all of them, for Claire will join them in the end—a holding environment, a shared space in which to endure, if not survive, the most unthinkable of all abandonments. And indeed, seated in the "holding environment" of the magic cave, the three *hold* hands. They are held and holding.

The importance of this flimsy little structure at the end of the film may be signaled by its absence from an earlier sequence. At the beginning of the film, amid the signs and portents of world destruction, we see Claire holding her son in her arms, sinking into the softened ground of the golf course green as she seems to try to hasten somewhere to save him. But this vision is not realized at the end of the film. Instead of being held by the mother, Leo is in a *holding environment* in which mother, son, and aunt hold hands. Is this the magic work of the magic cave? That it transitions Leo from being held to holding? When he is held by the mother in the opening sequence, the

boy, Leo, almost pubescent and clearly too large to be held, is infantilized. Here Claire is Winnicott's object-mother in relation to Leo. Perhaps the magic here is that Justine enters in to serve as Leo's environment-mother, and this is what enables the construction of the holding environment.

Either way, if we treat the opening sequence as Leo's dream (its dreamy, languorous tempo and its fantasy-like images suggest that this is a fair enough reading), then we may gain from applying Lear to von Trier, and not just the other way around. Recall that Plenty Coups, too, is a dreamer and that he dreams his way out of boyhood into manhood. Lear and the elders take that dream, which depicts a storm that leaves alive only a Chickadee and no Crow, to be a parable for the tribe. But Plenty Coups' dream is not only a parable for the tribe. It is also arguably a manhood dream, one that reassures a boy who must live out in the wild by himself for a few days that the small, too, can survive. Plenty Coups' dream teaches him that one need not be a full-grown Crow in order to survive a storm. Thus the dream eases the anxiety provoked by a manhood ritual's demand that a boy—a mere chickadee—take on manhood, unready.

If we take a similar approach to Leo's dream in *Melancholia* and treat it as a manhood ritual, too, we see that for him the anxiety is the opposite. Rather than fear being thrust into manhood, unready, Leo fears being held back; the mother who carries him like a baby when he is far too big for it is the mother who will not permit entry into (what is from her perspective, but possibly also from his) the catastrophe of mature masculine adulthood. The dream plays out the anxiety and informs the cure. From holding to holding environment, from infantilizing mother to playful aunt, from object-mother to environment-mother, from being held to holding hands, Leo in fantasy works through his fears and devises the magic of the magic cave—he builds a shared space, brings his object-mother and environment-mother together in an act of Winnicottian maturation, and reestablishes a relationship with his mother (either by using his playful aunt or by uniting the women).[52]

Might it be fair to say that "after that nothing happened"? Perhaps. But perhaps not. In so saying we would buy in, as James Martel argues, to teleology: "When a teleology is in place, nothing indeed can ever 'happen' because the teleology itself determines happening and it is all predestined." Real happening, the experience of event, is "only possible when we resist those teleologies," and refuse to buy in to "any sense of inevitability or fate." Thus,

anti-teleologists do what they can to make things happen (and making things happen is what Lear favors, after all, rather than merely going through motions). Lear sees Sitting Bull and Wraps His Tail as engaged in futility. But for Martel, they are the heroic "anti-teleologists" of Lear's story, "resisting a fate that they do not want in any way that they can." Following my reading of Von Trier's Leo as dreaming the end of the world and moving beyond it, Martel notes that in fact this youth, too, rejects the "certainties and absolutes" of teleology and that he does so by way of an object relation: "it takes a literalized object of anti-teleological force, an object-planet that mimics the inevitability of teleology to use that force as a weapon against itself." Rather than invoke contingency against teleology or try to restore the event, von Trier (or Leo) enlists the power of teleology against teleology. With what else might we stop the reproduction of the alienated everyday, which seems unstoppable, except by way of a planet that is implacable? (Perhaps this might perversely explain why, when Claire first sees the rogue planet, she says, "It looks friendly.") If the film's final crash is world-ending, that could mean that after that nothing happened. Or it could mean that after that, things finally started to happen again.

What should we make of the fact that the so-called magic cave of *Melancholia* looks like a burned out teepee, and echoes, rather magically, the cover of Lear's own book, published just a few years before? In *Everything That Rises: A Book of Convergences*, Lawrence Weschler notes "the degree to which images from the past create a context for ordering and approaching the chaos of the present."[53] That is, in contexts of catastrophe, such images

offer continuity, which reassures and pleases (psychologically and aestheti-
cally). "The place where you choose to stand and aim your camera and so
forth, the image you choose to take is a part of a history of images that
forms a reservoir of tropes in your head."[54] Joel Meyerowitz, whose photographs of New York City's 9/11 scene mirror classical art pieces (from
Millet's *The Gleaners* to Jasper Johns's *Three Flags*), responds: "Absolutely.
None of us are free of references. And when you grow up in the world of
art, things stick to you."[55] It is surely that stickiness that Lear is in quest of or,
and that von Trier, perhaps, chafes against, the possibility that, as Meyerowitz puts it, "a long tradition . . . has itself become part of you" and that you
can "see things through it that are identifiably yours."[56]

But every system of reference is also a kind of teleology—directed toward
an end, and therefore disavowing all alternatives as distraction (Lear on Sitting Bull, Wraps his Trail)—and such systems are also always constituted
by histories of theft and appropriation.[57] The teepee makes this clear. As teepee, it reassures, for it theologizes the present catastrophe, von Trier's end
of the world, intimating that we "deserve" it. We—living on native lands,
enjoying their riches—have it coming for past sins, crimes for which we
have never atoned, or passive profiting off of others' suffering. When in
von Trier's film three rich white people hold hands in a teepee and find
their way to each other, it is an act of cultural appropriation, but it is (also)
something else: chickens—or chickadees!—have come home to roost. The
teepee calls to them, to us, to bring us to our rightful end as our implication
in historical wrongs is avenged. This is theology, not theodicy. Or at least
that is one way to read it.

Alternatively, or also, von Trier's "magic cave" is arguably the movie theater in which many of us first held hands.[58] The movies were once screened
exclusively in public theaters. Constituting the event of public spectatorship,
they were also a scene of private intimacy.[59] Their capacity to do both, to
put us together with others, then turn out the lights and make us feel alone
with ourselves, is surely part of their magic. They *may* now be destined to
a destruction preordained by the digital revolution that some argue has
already made of the movies a ruin. Are new digital media forms the *diminution* of film, replacing the big screen giants of cinema and the collectivizing
experience of the cinematic spectacle with the small screen and the privatized, individuated—chickadee—experience it offers? We may see von

Trier's filmic monumentalism as an effort to forestall that by making pictures that are much too big for such small screens.

Interpreted as a mourning song for a meaningful life that has predeceased the destruction of the planet, von Trier's *Melancholia* depicts the catastrophe of planetary destruction as (1) the inevitable result of climate change and our seeming powerlessness to stop it, (2) a mere symptomatization of a prior unsuspected destruction of a once meaningful social order (at the hands of neoliberalism, in which case, Leo, like Plenty Coups, has dreamt his "tribe's" anxieties), and/or (3) the fantasy of a boy who dreams his way through an adolescence that feels world-ending because it involves aggression, anger, and other "ugly feelings" against the nuclear family (replaced in the end by an innovative alternative of mother-aunt—or Winnicott's two mothers: object-mother and environment-mother—in the magic cave).[60] These readings are connected because offsetting the destruction of late, neoliberal systemic capitalism will arguably take a certain amount of aggression.[61] Teleology must be fought with the force of a counter-teleology, if Martel is right. In any case, there is no way, as Justine says to Claire, for it to be "nice."[62]

Thus, we may also see the teepee as oriented toward a future, not the past. From this perspective, von Trier with this film is doing what a political theory of public things can appreciate about what Plenty Coups did: providing us with a public thing, let's call it the magic cave, and showing us the magic of its thingness. That it is the product of play is key, for the play enchants the object just as the object enchants the play.

On this reading, von Trier—whose film in so many ways parallels Lear's book—does two things that Lear's book does not. First, von Trier provides a critique of the path we have taken (the first readings, where the catastrophe is climate change or neoliberalism). Second, he provides an alternative maturation narrative that I suggested earlier is now needful, one in which dependency is not disavowed but owned and a new kind of future trajectory is imagined—one that moves not toward autonomy but toward interdependence. We are reminded by von Trier of our need for play, for intersubjective pleasures, and of the importance of shared or (in more democratic terms) *public* things to hold us and to be held and cared for by us, built and fought for by us. As we saw in Lecture Two, Winnicott would say that in such an environment we experience what feel like world-ending feelings, and we— and the world—survive. This requires that the things themselves survive.

In Winnicott's world, this is their magic. We destroy them and they survive, and they transfer their resilience to us. Survival can also mean rebirth or overlife—*sur-vivre*, in French. As William Connolly notes, our own moon was formed out of an earlier planetary collision.[63] Natality is often paired with destruction or mortality.

When Tocqueville observed that "The art of pursuing in common the objects of common desires [is democracy's] highest perfection," he had himself just recently witnessed the end of a world.[64] He would surely agree that this art postulates something like Lear's radical hope, which, as Lear says, "is a daunting form of commitment to a goodness in the world that transcends one's current ability to grasp what it is."[65] But Lear throws us back on ourselves in a way, I want to say. To him, the task of hope is an individual task, a mark of a person's courage, not a task of collective politics (which calls for a different courage). Ethics, not politics, is Lear's domain, as is indicated by his subtitle: "Ethics in the Face of Cultural Devastation." The focus on the power of an individual (taken up by tribal leaders, on my account, but on Lear's still oriented around Plenty Coups' singular radical hope) is the outcome of Lear's focus on catastrophe. But what if the real catastrophe is the very individual on whom he focuses?

The catastrophe relevant to us now, that is, is not just that of ethnic cleansing, like the Holocaust, which Lear has in mind throughout his book as an analogy. It is the catastrophe of capitalism in a neoliberal context, and its attendant modes of individuation, alienation, overwork, and desolation. In this latter catastrophe, the individual is increasingly alone, networked, and isolated, our powers pathologized as aggression, and the holding environments that enable us collectively to make and contest meaning are attenuated. We are exposed, like the ruined single teepee on which both these "texts" converge, without skin. We are vulnerable yet responsible for the world (in Winnicott's and Arendt's senses), in need of it, but often feeling powerless to defend it. Lear wants to show how we can be the bridge to our own permanence. But this overinvestment in individual capacities cannot just be the solution, since it is also the problem.[66]

Besides, I would note, the elders are always there in his book, reported on if not thematized.[67] Without their communal acts of dream interpretation, the dream that Plenty Coups dreams would remain just his. It might get him through his time in the woods, but it could not become the tribe's dream, it would not hold their anxieties, it would not provide a way for the tribe to survive, or become complicit in, their own destruction. Similarly, Leo's dream takes on significance only when he makes it real with his aunt, Justine, or when his aunt takes him up and enters into its realization. Their skinless teepee is fragile but the bonds of play, interpretation, mutuality, and mentorship that produce it are sturdy. Their collaborative play, we may say, is a working through. And the trio's hand-holding, which represents Winnicott's "between" and Arendt's "in-between," is enabled by the holding environment Leo and his aunt have built together, even if—or especially because—it has no skin.[68] It is a ruin. But sometimes the ruin speaks.

The tribal elders in Lear's book, like the Greek tragedies' Chorus, create the meaning, read the omens, interpret the signs, manage the community, and use parable and allegory to create a holding environment that makes life and not just survival possible. As Lear explains further in an essay published after *Radical Hope*,[69] when tribe members returned from fighting for the U.S. Army in the Second World War, they were asked to tell their war stories. Tell us what happened, the tribal elders said, and they listened. As Joe Medicine Crow reported of his own experience telling the story of his exploits, the elders celebrated him, saying: You counted coup! And you have "completed the four requirements to become chief."[70] (Counting coup was a ritual of war in the old days, before white conquest.) The Crow fighter had not thought of himself as counting coup, a practice that had died out seventy years earlier. Relating his wartime experiences became a platform on which to reanimate the old Crow practice for which Plenty Coups himself had been named. Importantly, also, though Lear does not note it, the elders were offering the returning soldier a Winnicottian "holding environment," constructing it for him and for the tribe out of the ruins of war and ritual. Listening, mirroring, narrating, hosting, receiving, they sew a skin for the teepee, and build a future out of a ruined past. Thus, they provide a frame in relation to which the violence that may disturb the young man's soul becomes not his undoing, but an aggression that can be collectively borne and owned: It is part of a Crow tradition of manly exploits that precedes him by centuries and to which he now belongs.

Lear disagrees with this reading, which he anticipates, because it "collaborate[s] in covering over the trauma the Crow had to endure."[71] And he is right. That is a risk of this reading—that it papers over the rupture in intelligibility wrought by conquest. This is no mere repurposing of older concepts, no updating to remain the same (to borrow the title of a recent book by Wendy Chun). It is, Lear says, more like a "resurrection of a concept that had fallen into a moribund state." The distinction matters if what is wanted is a philosophical reflection on the intelligibility and the conditions of its violation (Lear's topic in this essay). It may not matter as much if what we are after is some account of how experiences that are unbearable can be borne if they are mediated by public things, held in a holding environment by others who assign meanings to them. Do the tribal elders paper over a break? Or do they ransack what remains of their repertoire as Crow to provide what they can to men who need it?

The function of the Chorus and the tribal elders is that assigned by Winnicott to the "ordinary devoted mother": to absorb the aggression and pain of the developing child, take it out of play or channel it on behalf of the collective.[72] But it is only when we partner Lear with von Trier that the elders' role as Chorus becomes clear. Why? Because, by contrast with Lear's focus on the dauntless individual, von Trier gives us the magic cave, and that shared or public thing points us toward new formations of traditional collectivity and new forms of kinship. (It is notable, for example, that the family of three in the film's closing shot is made up of two sisters and their child. There is no father in this iterative copy of the nuclear family; just Winnicott's two mothers, united by the son who is precisely at what Winnicott calls "the humpty-dumpty stage" of development.)[73] Here to be hopeful is to insist on the importance of the held hands and not on the courage of a radical individual with radical hope. Here courage is a trait of intersubjective alliance and not the individual virtue in the name of which such alliances have all too often been not only forged but also broken.

For von Trier, the teepee may connote only a ruin. But does that ruin point to a destroyed past that is now our fully fated future? Or does it connote a ruin that may yet point to a different future, a "survival," to borrow Michael Oakeshott's term, that may reopen the future in ways not entirely determined by what has passed and was once cast as inexorable?[74] Perhaps the teepee's capacity to pose these questions to us, and to scramble the teleologies and temporalities of progress and maturation that surround and constitute us, are what make the magic cave magical. Perhaps there is power, after all, in the teepee that seems useless—no more than a house built of sticks—in the face of catastrophe. Built in play, perhaps it might meet the democratic need or at least stand for the need to meet it.

Where Dickinsonian hope never asks anything of us ("never—in Extremity, It asked a crumb—of me") and radical hope accepts thinning out in response to pressure, the democratic need for public things demands to be met. The democratic need worries that thinning is now a neoliberal tactic and calls instead for a thickening that refurnishes the world with the things we have lately dispensed with. The democratic needs calls upon us to provide and secure public things around which to constellate, by which to be gathered together, over which to be divided, in relation to which to be interpellated—as equals. Notwithstanding the proud history of conscientious objection with which U.S. democracy in particular has been associated, democracy as such is opposed to the opt-out and insists on the all-in. Or, perhaps better, we can say, as I noted in Lecture One, that conscientious objection postulates the all-in in a way that opting out does not. The aim of conscientious objection, after all, is—or ought to be—to rejoin a better public thing, not to destroy it or leave it stranded.

That future may take any of many forms. Recall that in Lecture One I discussed Wendy Brown's lament for the contemporary Left's seeming lack of interest in sovereignty. We may find it among First Peoples, or among food sovereignty movements, I suggested. Asking, with this in mind, "What is the teepee in von Trier?" we must answer: A ruin? A sign of the inevitable destruction that awaits us all? An image of the justness of what awaits us, given what we have meted out to others, remorselessly? Or might it be a sign of a future to be celebrated and built, in which our dwellings are more open to nature or at least not fortressed against it, and in which we risk experiencing each other in conflict and through play, collaboration, and touch? The bare teepee, that is to say, surely represents an old near-genocide; but might it also, without remediating that past, incite a new, skinless future of thinging out loud?

Public Things, Shared Space, and the Commons

Things do not come with transitional guarantees. Some may thwart and others will facilitate our development or activities, but regardless, holding environments are part of the infrastructure of human development and of the active human life. We may infer that holding environments are necessary, in particular, to *democratic* life, especially if we extend Winnicott's and Arendt's accounts to think specifically in terms of *public* things.

An image presses itself on me as I write this; three, actually, three iconic images of Marian Anderson performing at the Lincoln Memorial. Looked at in sequence, they seem to represent the Arendt/Winnicott trajectory—from held to holding to action in concert—all in relation to a public thing. The object does not change in these images but Anderson's relation to it, *our* relation to it, does.

The occasion of these first two images is this: In 1939, the Daughters of the American Revolution (DAR) denied Marian Anderson the use of Constitution Hall for a performance. The great African American vocalist,

Thomas D. McAvoy/The LIFE Picture Collection/Getty Images

Thomas D. McAvoy/The LIFE Picture Collection/Getty Images

whose "haunting, impassioned singing prompted the great maestro Arturo Toscanini to proclaim, 'A voice like yours is heard once in 100 years,'" performed instead at the Lincoln Memorial for an integrated audience.[1] Eleanor Roosevelt, First Lady at the time and until then a member of the DAR—she resigned over this[2]—helped arrange the free concert, held on Easter Sunday, 1939, and attended by over 75,000 people. Walter White, then executive secretary of the National Association for the Advancement of Colored People (NAACP), had suggested an outdoor venue, perhaps to facilitate attendance by an integrated audience. Since the Lincoln Memorial was a national monument, Secretary of the Interior Harold Ickes was also involved in the planning.[3] Photographs of the event depict Anderson from one angle as if she were seated in Lincoln's great lap, held by him; from another angle, she can be seen holding together a great crowd with her presence.[4] Handled and held. Holding. She opened with "My Country, 'Tis of Thee." As she sang, she emphasized the words liberty and freedom, and

"instead of 'of thee I sing' she sang 'to thee we sing.'"[5] In so doing, she and everyone there made of the Lincoln Memorial, a public thing, a live holding environment for democratic citizenship and action in concert.

Twenty-four years later, Anderson appeared again on the same stage at the 1963 March on Washington, a photograph of which actually combines the handling and holding here noted but goes beyond them. In this image, Anderson is surrounded by others on stage, and Lincoln is almost obscured, his lap invisible; the monumental size of his statue is diminished.[6] He is now one among others, part of an African American collective action, *absorbed into* an action in concert whose fundamental traits are, on Arendt's account, equality and plurality.

The Lincoln Memorial is the sort of thing Arendt has in mind as the basis of shared memory and action in *The Human Condition*. If I have in these lectures focused on public things and not on the commons or shared space, it is partly due to her influence, but it is not my intent to rule out the latter two. A political theory of public things draws on all three, though admittedly the other two may not always be happy about that. From the perspective of the commons, which names the losses exacted by long histories of dispossession, appropriation, and accumulation, public things may well look like one more enclosure in a very long line of them. Replacing antagonism with unity, the language of publicness disguises the class conflicts to which talk of the commons calls attention. (Critical accounts of Lincoln as an imperial president are an example of the contributiveness of such perspectives.) Talk of public things only obscures the thefts that the language of the commons seeks to commemorate and reverse. In sum, the charge is that public things are an ideological fiction: the "public" is a phantom and their "thingness" (by way of which air, water, and land are commodified) is a ruse.

It is a powerful critique and one thing to be said in response is that there is truth in it (though thingness need not necessarily be reduced to commodification). It is true that public things, as I have argued throughout, may well be the results of prior thefts and appropriations, which in the United States are often driven more by race than class, or both. For example, the federal highway system was used, sometimes quite intentionally, to break up minority communities and redistribute land. President Obama's secretary of transportation, Anthony Foxx, recently made the point. As the *Washington Post* reports, "Foxx, only the third African-American to ever hold the top federal transportation policy job, is explicitly acknowledging and condemning a history of destroying black communities and stealing wealth from their residents through intentional [infrastructure] decisions."[7]

The dispossessions in question are not all from the distant past: In the 1980s, the government of St. Louis bought (some said coercively) middle-class blacks out of their residences in Kinloch, Missouri, in order to expand a nearby airport. Hundreds of millions of dollars were said to be at stake for investors, business, and the city, and everyone would benefit from improved air quality as a result of more efficient use of expanded airport runways. Aside from cleaner air, though, other public things were also at stake, but they went unmentioned: "for the state's longest-standing black city, its bakeries and drugstores and public schools, the project spelled doom. After a series of buyouts that locals say felt more like arm-twisting than a genuine personal choice to stay or sell, Kinloch's population plunged from over 4,000 to below 300."

The punch line: "Many of them, most of them, ended up moving to a town called Ferguson." The promised profits never materialized.

Stories like this may help account for the appeal of anti-statism shared by both the shared space and commons models, the former on behalf of an anarcho-libertarianism that promotes free individual agency and/or markets and the latter on behalf of the commons betrayed by enclosure-style policies to this day. Of the two, the commons is more avowedly anti-market in its approach (the commons identifies "resources that should not be alienated for market use, but should remain non-propertized and 'owned' . . . by everyone")—and the shared space model is less so.[8] It is notable, indeed, that from the perspective of the commons, Arendt's association of the natural world with Labor and not Work or Action can suddenly seem like a way to protect the commons from usurpation.

The story does not end with exposé, but with repair. One comment made by Foxx points us *toward* public things, not away from them, in spite of their history. Laying out the critique of the unjust politics of infrastructure, Foxx made clear that "the agency wants to make up for it now." The way to do that is to do "better at balancing needed infrastructure expansions with the interests of local communities," and that, paradoxically, may require more federal government stewardship over state-level spending of federal funds on infrastructure.

I have used the term *public things* loosely, to cover more than those things that are provided by the state and secured by its sovereignty. Public things include the local or the regional, and even many that are—in terms of funding—hybrid public and private. This may look, to advocates of the commons or shared space, like it lessens the critical leverage of the term. But the term *public things*, unlike the commons and shared space, helps out when the aim is to explore the possible contributions that public *thingness* has to make to democratic life and subjectivity.

Public things are one of *democracy*'s necessary conditions, I argued in Lecture One, and without them democratic life is not just impoverished but unsustainable. If democratic theorists neglect public things, we end up theorizing the demos or proceduralism without the things that give them purpose and whose adhesive and integrative powers are necessary to the perpetual reformation of democratic collectivity. If we focus only on shared space or the commons, we get either a more individualistic political subject than the subject of public things or one that is less so. We also dispense with state institutions rather than dedicate ourselves to retaking them or, as in the case of Foxx, repurposing or rededicating them to their properly public pursuits. That said, shared space and commons-oriented approaches share with a political theory of public things a disposition to call attention to the scenes and not just the subjects of democratic life.[9]

In any case, all three models have contributions to make to the project of preventing ever-increasing privatization and furthering the quest for justice and equality in contemporary democratic societies. These three models coexist and their coexistence, at its best, is agonistic, not sphereist or pluralist. That is to say, we do well to turn to each of these three models of collective or collected living—shared space, the commons (or undercommons),[10] and public things—to subject the others to critical interrogation and judgment by its own standards, while also enlisting the others' support for ends on which the different models converge. From the perspective of the commons, we see how the state—itself supposedly and potentially a public thing—is captured by various interests, how it is enlisted to police and subsidize public/private hybrids that are more private than public, how its hierarchical structure may betray the democracy it claims to vouchsafe. With my emphasis throughout on action in concert, I hope it has been clear that taking the state seriously as a democratic political resource does not mean displacing the central importance to public things of agonistic action in concert. From the perspective of shared space, as I shall argue, we see how public things *depend* on being agonistically taken and retaken by concerted action. They depend on civic care, concern, hope, and play as much as we depend on their permanence and vice versa. And from the perspective of public things, we apprehend the adhesive and integrative powers of things and the dependence of all collecteds—not just of citizens and publics but also of crowds and commons—on things and their powers of enchantment.

Admittedly, for some theorists of the commons, this enchantment may be an unwelcome spell from which we need to awaken. I do not disagree. As I noted in the Introduction and Lecture One, criticisms of public things as falsely universal, falsely inclusive, colonial, appropriative, and statist have been tremendously important and apt. In their wake, many of us can now only experience many state-supported public things with ambivalence, at best. This may affect how we relate to already existing public things but it is not a reason to oppose public things, as such, or to be reluctant to claim and mobilize their powers now, or to shrink from building new ones. Nor is it a reason to conflate public things with state sovereignty, which these days is just one of the mechanisms of their reproduction and can be one of the mechanisms of their betrayal.

I have tried here to make the case for the contributions of public things to progressive politics at a time when the energies of the Left in political theory's critical literature tend to be anti-statist or anti-sovereigntist. This at a moment when a great deal of indigenous activism is rightly and understandably, in my view, claiming sovereignty and the rights, autonomy, and resources that go with it. My claim throughout has been that the state itself is a public thing worth fighting for (and Foxx is a great example of this), but I have also emphasized the importance of other public things, some claimed by the commons—air, water, earth, in Arendt's domain of Labor—and some part of the infrastructure of modern life—sewage, universities, libraries, reservoirs, in Arendt's domain of Work. In addition, I have underlined the importance of the counterbalancing powers of other affiliations and modes of activism for those living in or in relation to the state system—that is, all of us. At its best, democratic life involves us in a variety of more or less egalitarian relationships to a variety of public or shared things, including even those forms of life that are sometimes called withdrawalist. These last build alternative publics, public spheres, and public things, which may vivify our imaginings of alternative ways of living. Their enactment of alternative sovereignties, even in their not fully realized forms, can inform future activism.[11]

It is worth noting that the adhesive and attachment effects of public things, suggested by the analogy to Winnicott's transitional objects and the things of Arendt's Work, surely apply to the experience of the commons or shared space, as well. So there is no necessary zero-sumness here. A political theory of public things need not be exclusive; it supports plural forms of collaborative tending to shared and common concerns. Together, all three models counter the push to privatization and offer alternatives to the fantasy of security through segregated use and to the romance of private, heroic entrepreneurship. But, as their critical perspectives on each other indicate, the three models are not necessarily always compatible and should not be assumed to be so. Certain orientations to common holdings will sometimes feed a commitment to public things, sometimes not.

I turn now to a Dutch traffic engineer named Hans Monderman, whose idea of *shared space* is actually a critique of public things, which Monderman associates narrowly with state bureaucratic and technocratic management. Monderman was frustrated by the focus of most traffic engineers on car accidents and accident prevention. That focus promotes the idea of the street as a dangerous site of vulnerability for pedestrians and cyclists and puts cars at the top of a traffic hierarchy. Signs of this mentality, Monderman argued, are raised curbs, demarcated walkways, and fencing at busy intersections, all of which discipline pedestrians to move only in certain ways and at certain times lest they put themselves at risk by stepping into the pathways of cars. Other signs of the problem are signs themselves, the routinely ubiquitous signage that posts where cars may go, and where not, and at what speed. The more signs, Monderman liked to say, the less trust in the people who are using the space and who ought to be choreographing their own use of it. Monderman was highly alert to the potentially normalizing effects of public things organized in these ways. They not only route our passage through shared space, which is all they *claim* to do, but they also cultivate habits of obedience that Winnicott associates with "shop window faces," faces belonging to those who suffer a loss of self and spontaneity.

Comparing traffic intersections with ice skating arenas, Monderman pointed out that no signs are posted for skaters on the ice: Skaters are free to go in different directions and use the space in a variety of ways, and they all manage to share the space. Monderman's faith in the ability of people to self-regulate, adjust, reorganize, and accommodate each other without rules that tell them what to do is virtually anarchistic. So is his belief in the power of good design to promote such autonomy and the power of bad design to thwart it.[12]

Possibly channeling Hayek and the idea of spontaneous self-organization, possibly representing the sorts of anarchism for which James Scott offers "two cheers," Monderman observed that people are good at organizing their own behavior; they can be trusted.[13] When traditional traffic engineers protect people from risk, they not only inhibit people's autonomy, they also prevent their random meeting. Long before the post 9/11 security debates, Monderman was interested in what he called "the hidden costs of safety."

His critique of civil servants is a critique of a certain style of governing. The civil servant he criticizes is a product of an Enlightenment mentality that rules over public space and regulates its use as a public thing from above. The alternative that Monderman promotes is that of shared space, the rules for its occupation and use come from below, and its operations are more like those of a hive than a regiment. Rather than respect the one brain of the civil servant, the shared space model respects the many brains of its users, who swarm together and sort out their conflicts.[14] They become less dependent on government and on leaders and more able to sort out context-appropriate solutions to problems.[15] What goes unsaid, though, is that in such environments, minorities may find themselves marginalized—or worse—by a majority's well-working hive. What also goes unsaid—and may be a response to the first concern—is that all of this depends on designing shared space otherwise and those redesigns depend on an expert too. They depend, as Monderman would surely be the first to say, on a different kind of traffic engineer, a different approach to traffic engineering.

The shared space model levels the street and sidewalks, removing fencing and traffic lights, and uses more subtle signs like changes in materials (such as brick to stone pavers) to signal various uses of the street, but without separating in any regulated way cars from pedestrians from bikes. There are no traffic signals but there is a host of subtle suggestions that the space in this area is shared and that appropriate—but unspecified—measures should be taken. Areas that were once forbidding to pedestrians are now experienced as navigable because the status of the various parties in shared space—cars, bikes, and pedestrians—is leveled. When all this works, motorists slow down. They do not need signs or the threat of ticketing to tell them to do so; they respect the pace of shared space. The result is a plaza or a square that looks less like an intersection and more like an ice skating rink full of skaters, some upright, others using sleds, chairs, or barrels. Monderman doesn't note it, but one thing that makes all this work is local knowledge. The cues offered up in the shared space model assume some familiarity with the way people live in the area. Or they assume the power of the crowd to set expectations for those who do not.

One of the things that clearly delighted Monderman was how people asserted ownership of shared space. He did not seem to worry too much about what was public and what was private. There is a hybrid quality to shared space; he was open always to various kinds of squatting, appropriating, taking. In one of his lectures he showed a picture of a single table and chairs put outside by a pub owner, eager to extend into a newly built plaza, a new shared space, or a public thing. Monderman was not concerned that this private business was improperly taking over what ought to be a public domain. As he saw it, the owner was "claiming" the space and in so doing showed that he knew what the space was *for*. Monderman saw the move as playful. We might do well to worry that what begins with a table and chair could end with privatization of spaces that were once available for shared use. Public use of public space will soon have to be paid for, if that table remains and if others follow. But Monderman would have counted on other users of shared space to make that point. It is their task to play back, to make the next move. This is the agonism in his anarchism.

To be clear, the idea of shared space is not an adequate remedy for the many contemporary exploitations and inequalities to which democratic politics must respond, for which we are often responsible, and in which we are implicated. But the documented capacity of humans socialized into regulated public space to adapt to shared space may inspire democratic theorists looking for still more alternatives to settled ideas about how best to preserve and extend concern for public affairs and how to regulate shared living in democratic settings, especially in the context of specifically neoliberal pressures to privatize as a one-size-fits-all solution to every political challenge. Most important, from the perspective of public things, Monderman's way of thinking about shared space offers an agonistic-anarchistic orientation to public things that is attractively different from deliberative and liberal approaches that would (if they attended to public things at all) likely seek to regulate and preserve such things—and provide norms for that—rather than risk entrusting them without regulation to the public(s) they have the power to interpellate. To say the view is "attractively different" does not mean it should replace the others. But it should prove a useful supplement or disturbance to them.

What we learn from looking at public things in relation to shared space and the commons is that the public things model is one institutional formation or expression of common holding in democratic life. That same model therefore will betray the common holdings, to which it—just like any other model—can only give partial expression. Each possible expression or institutional formation elicits different inhabitations of citizenship, different ways of knowing and acting, different subjectivities and different object relations. The relish with which Monderman explains the shared space model suggests he knows he is not just talking about traffic but is rather—or also—developing a vernacular for citizenship that emphasizes egalitarianism and mutuality. Clearly, Monderman hopes that the result will be a diminution of self-absorption, less focus on security, and the emergence of something like care, concern, collaboration, and play in shared space settings. In sum, the shared space model, and Monderman himself, serve as Winnicott's good enough (m)other, for this is a holding environment that Monderman describes, a site in which object relations support individuation, invention, and collaboration.

In 2014, the San Francisco Recreation and Park Service began selling reserved time slots for the use of a public park. A passerby filmed a confrontation between new-to-the-neighborhood tech workers and the local teens whose play they interrupted one day. In response to the request that they clear the field, which the tech workers said they had reserved online, the local teens showed they knew what a park is *for*: They invited the tech workers to join in their game. They can be heard saying "come play pick-up with us!"[16] The tech workers' response was to display their piece of paper, evidence that they paid $27 for the hour of private use. This alteration of the public thing into a rentable resource by local government is transformative. It does not just kick some kids off their field. When public things are subject to private rental, our entire relationship to them is changed. Henceforth, instead of arriving at the playground, sizing others up, figuring out how to be invited in to join a game already in play, or waiting our turn, the new mores of the new scene position us to ask: Who has the right to the place? Do they have a piece of paper that means I can't or can play? Whose side will be taken when the police are called? When the locals welcomed the tech workers in to the public thing, the public thing had already been hijacked. The change was not irreversible, however. Perhaps the YouTube video helped: later that same year, in September 2014, it was reported that: "After public uproar, SF Rec & Park removed the policy that allowed this encounter to happen."[17] Public uproar is, in this instance, the action in concert on which public things depend and which they help generate. Public things are the world-stabilizing infrastructure on which our capacity to act in concert depends, and by which we may also be thwarted.

These days, as in this case, states are often the generators of privatization, seeking revenues they can no longer raise through taxation, now that new taxation in the United States seems to have been—for the moment, anyway—ruled out as an option. But state institutions can also be defenders of the public thing against privatization. State centralization may have generated traffic engineers with the top-down mentalities Monderman excoriated. But states can also support more context-sensitive styles of design. In Columbus, Ohio, "Interstate construction left communities literally walled off from the city's business hub for decades. But last summer [in 2015], the city officially opened a grass-lined car, pedestrian, and bike bridge over I-71 that stitches the highway wound closed and reconnects people to opportunity."[18] How things go—whether or not they move in reparative directions—depends partly on the concerted action of citizens and partly on judicial and electoral politics.

Another example: Food and Water Watch (FWW) appealed to the Oregon governor's office for years, in the hope of gaining support for its opposition to the appropriation of public water in Oregon by Nestlé. It was to no avail. Said FWW, "Since 2008, we had submitted tens of thousands of public comments to state agencies. According to then-Governor Kitzhaber's staff, they received more letters, emails and phone calls on this issue than any other in Oregon." But the governor did not take action, and activists finally chose a different and more direct route. In May 2016, with 69 percent of the vote, they won a ballot measure making it illegal to bottle water. The efficacy of the measure will now depend partly on the enforcement powers of the state.[19] And those powers will be exercised or not depending partly on the follow-up of the activists who got the ballot passed. The power of state institutions is not a resource to be casually discarded by the progressive Left. We chafe at it when it works against us. We find ways around it when necessary. Why not enlist it to work for us in an agonistic politics of public things? That power is what is at stake for those seeking to repair democratic forms of life. Stefano Harney and Fred Moten criticize the "dispersal and deputisation of state violence." Perhaps we could use that as an indication that *we* may act as agents of dispersal and deputization with regard to public things, and in that way stand our ground.[20]

ACKNOWLEDGMENTS

Thanks to the Thinking Out Loud committee, the late Helen Tartar, and Dimitris Vardoulakis for the invitation to "think out loud" as part of the Thinking Out Loud Series, hosted by the University of Western Sydney in Sydney, Australia. Charles Barbour served as discussant at the live events, and I appreciate his taking time away from his own work to comment insightfully on my early formulations. Anna Terwiel helped prepare the manuscript for publication and provided great research assistance for the lectures, which have undergone substantial revision since I gave them in Sydney in 2013. The Preface, Lecture One, and Epilogue are almost entirely new material, which I added to the lectures in the fall of 2015 and then revised in the spring of 2016 after receiving readers' reports from Fordham University Press. Lecture Two, likewise, is almost entirely new—an extensively revised combination of the original Lectures One and Two given at the live events. And Lecture Three is a much-revised version of the original third lecture. In the three years between lectures and book, with the project still developing, I published parts of the project as articles in *Political Concepts* ("Resilience"), *Political Theory* ("What Kind of Thing Is Land? Hannah Arendt's Object Relations, or: The Jewish Unconscious of Arendt's Most 'Greek' Text"), and *Political Research Quarterly* ("Public Things"), but the book has moved quite a distance from these earlier efforts. Publication details are in the Bibliography.

I want to thank Fordham University Press, and especially Richard Morrison, for waiting patiently for nearly three years as I reworked my lectures less quickly than anticipated, subtracting material, adding material, and rethinking some issues. I am grateful also to Bruce Robbins and one other anonymous reader for the Press, whose generous responses to the project gave me the perspective I needed for the final round of revisions. Although I have extensively revised and tightened the argument for the book, I have tried to preserve the feel of the work as lectures, in the spirit of the invitation to "think out loud," and with the aim of preserving the feel of the live events in 2013. This means I've permitted myself to write, at times, in a more speculative way than I might normally do: to think out loud, this time in writing. I hope this makes what follows more accessible than the typical monograph.

I am grateful to Amanda Anderson for suggesting that the "public things" project in which I had become entangled was really two books, thus helping me to see, finally, how to finish this one and move on to the next. Thanks to Brown University for the research and other leaves that helped me finish this book and start the next, and to the Haffenreffer Museum of Anthropology, which supports research in Native Studies and awarded me a faculty fellowship in 2015–16. And thanks to my incredible network of readers and interlocutors, whose work I read and who make time to read mine, even though we are all too busy. In particular, for their contagious enthusiasm and brilliant commentary on parts of this manuscript, I am grateful to James Martel, Miriam Leonard, Jason Frank, George Shulman, and Lori Marso. I am also indebted to John Seery, whom I have known the longest of all, and who did me the favor of organizing a manuscript workshop on this book (in penultimate draft) in the spring of 2016 with some of his wonderful students at Pomona College.

Finally, I want to thank Australia's ABC television station for televising the first lecture, and the Australia Broadcast Corporation for broadcasting all three of the original lectures on the radio. I note that much of the best work of D. W. Winnicott, an inspiration for these lectures, appeared first as radio lectures in Britain, broadcast during the Second World War and after. Then, too, there was a public, noncommercial station available to broadcast such noncommercial work, later gathered as lectures into publication as a book.

INTRODUCTION: THINGING OUT LOUD

1. Bruno Latour, "From Realpolitik to Dingpolitik, or How to Make Things Public," in *Making Things Public: Atmospheres of Democracy*, ed. Bruno Latour and Peter Weibel (Cambridge, Mass.: MIT Press, 2005), 5.

2. Hannah Arendt, *The Human Condition* (Chicago: University of Chicago Press, 1998), 9.

3. Ludwig Wittgenstein, *Philosophical Investigations*, trans. G. E. M. Anscombe (Oxford: Blackwell, 1953), 141–142.

4. For Winnicott, as for other psychoanalytic thinkers, object relations refers first and primarily to the mother, an object for the infant. I take my bearings in this book, however, from the object relations to transitional objects that, in Winnicott, are things—things like blankets, teddy bears, and so on that become saturated with meaning and affect by the infant's or child's relation to them.

5. I focus on their convergences, because that is one of this project's contributions, but Winnicott's objects have more agency and recalcitrance (not just resilience) than Arendt's things, as we shall see.

6. The rhetoric of privatization obscures from view the many partnerships of government and business in our neoliberal context (subsidies, bailouts, incentives, tax breaks, policing, and so on) while advertising other partnerships explicitly—business and government working together in hybrid ventures.

7. That history is proudly reported in precisely these nationalist terms at goo.gl/8lcpn4.

8. In *Red Skin, White Masks: Rejecting the Colonial Politics of Recognition* (Minneapolis: University of Minnesota Press, 2014), Glen Coulthard names problems of "infrastructure" as falsely public.

9. In part for this reason, some are calling for universities to be "undercommoned," a call noted in the Epilogue.

10. This may have already happened, more or less. A symptom of that reduction of democratic life to repetitive private work and exceptional public emergencies in contemporary neoliberal contexts is the prominence of mourning in recent years in Left political theory and cultural studies. I have written elsewhere about that turn, contrasting its focus on the mortal with a more Arendtian emphasis on the natal. See *Antigone, Interrupted* (Cambridge: Cambridge University Press, 2013).

11. Christopher Breu, *Insistence of the Material: Literature in the Age of Biopolitics* (Minneapolis: University of Minnesota Press, 2014). See also Benjamin R. Barber, "The Art of Public Space: Filling the Empty Streets and Turning Pedestrian Piazzas into True Commons," *The Nation*, August 12, 2009.

12. There is a growing critical literature on the topic, in which concerns are expressed about the effects of privatization on everything from local political autonomy and accountability to "place attachment" and neighborhood effects. See, for example, Anna Minton, *What Kind of World Are We Building? The Privatisation of Public Space* (London: Royal Institute of Chartered Surveyors, 2006), citing Ebenezer Howard's "inspirational garden city movement" and the "concept of Community Land Trusts" as well as "affordable planning policies" as movements, organizations, and policies to be furthered. Place attachment is arguably a political corollary to Winnicott's exploration of healthy attachment in infancy. On the hidden costs of privatization, "A new report from the Colorado Center for Policy Studies out of the University of Colorado outlines the true price of outsourcing government functions like sanitation and healthcare: weakened social infrastructure, deepened economic inequity and hollowed-out civic institutions" (goo.gl/ybbMB2). Also of concern are the marketing and policing of new private or hybrid (BID) spaces as clean and safe, where "clean and safe" often means restricting access to public space to those who pass certain racially or economically marked standards: e.g., no hoodies allowed.

13. Efficiency is not democracy's only value. We miss this when we think only about things like "service delivery" (though a democracy's effective and fair delivery of services is important, too; the worry here is what happens when efficiency becomes *the* standard, and not just one among many, for assessing public things). Efficiency may not even be a value at all, at least not for democracies that are, as Winnicott might say, "in health."

14. As Bruce Robbins points out: "Along with the line separating those who do and don't have easily affordable access to clean water, the line between those who have and those who don't have a proper sewage disposal system is arguably the most important political line in the world today." Robbins, "The

Smell of Infrastructure: Notes toward an Archive," *boundary 2* 34, no. 1 (2007): 33.

15. Elaine Scarry, *Thinking in an Emergency* (New York: Norton, 2011); and see my discussion of the book in "Three Models of Emergency Politics," *boundary 2* 4, no. 2 (2014).

16. Libby Sander and Susan Saulny, "Bridge Collapse in Minneapolis Kills at Least 7," *New York Times*, August 2, 2007.

17. Audra Simpson points this out in *Mohawk Interruptus: Political Life across the Borders of Settler States* (Durham, N.C.: Duke University Press, 2014), chapter 6. It is a key point in the film *Kanehsatake: 270 Years of Resistance*, directed by Alanis Obomsawin (1993), at https://www.youtube.com/watch?v=7yP3srFvhKs.

18. On the background issue of the collapse of the Meech Lake Accord, see Larry Kusch, Mia Rabson, Mary Agnes Welch, and Bruce Owen, "25 Years Ago, a Simple 'No': Elijah Harper Becomes Indigenous Hero for his Role in Meech Lake," *Winnipeg Free Press*, May 6, 2015.

19. In both Volumes I and II he associates this with the first settlers: "at the time of the first immigrations, local government, that fertile germ of free institutions, had already taken deep root in English ways." *Democracy in America*, trans. George Lawrence, ed. J. P. Mayer (New York: Perennial Classics, 2001), 1:33. Again, in Volume II, he says that they arrived schooled in jury duty and political deliberation.

20. Might ADD be the symptomatic disorder of neoliberalism?

21. Alexis de Tocqueville, *Democracy in America*, trans. Henry Reeve (Cambridge, Mass.: Sever and Francis, 1898), 536.

22. Ibid., 538.

23. Ibid., 435–436, 448. Also quoted in "Trail of Tears," in *The Encyclopedia of Native American Legal Tradition*, ed. Bruce Elliott Johansen (Westport, Conn.: Greenwood Press, 1998), 329.

24. The earth appears as an agent of vengeance in Aeschylus's *Libation Bearers*:

What can atone for blood
once fallen on the ground?
Alas for the grief-filled hearth
Alas for the buried home! . . .
The nurturing earth drinks blood,
she drinks her fill. That gore,
which cries out for revenge,
will not disappear or seep away.

Aeschylus, *The Oresteia*, trans. Ian Johnston (Arlington, Va.: Richer Resources Publications, 2007), 60–90.

104 Notes to pages 11–14

25. The fragility of things is also the title of a recent book by William Connolly on related themes and in which he develops his own compelling reading of von Trier's *Melancholia*.

LECTURE ONE. DEMOCRACY'S NECESSARY CONDITIONS

1. One exception is Benjamin Barber: "The ancient agora, or civic market-place, of democratic Athens and the covered arcades of nineteenth-century European towns exemplify a spirit where public things (literally *res publica*, the origin of our word 'republic') become paramount. Entertainment and commerce are necessary and important, but they 'work' because people are drawn into public spaces for other reasons: to play in the company of others, to watch one another and see others with fresh vision . . . to interact with strangers, to get out of private space and into common space." Benjamin Barber, "The Art of Public Space: Filling the Empty Streets and Turning Pedestrian Piazzas into True Commons," *The Nation*, August 12, 2009. Another is Ella Myers, *Worldly Ethics: Democratic Politics and Care for the World* (Durham, N.C.: Duke University Press, 2013). Myers's topic is not public things, but rather the broader category "world," which she draws from Hannah Arendt and which encompasses what Arendt calls "a 'physical in-between' and a 'second subjective in-between' that is constituted by 'deeds and words'" (Myers, 89–90, citing *The Human Condition*, 52). For this reason, Myers does not attend especially to the Work chapter of *The Human Condition*, which I argue here is central to a consideration of public things.

2. Wendy Brown, *Undoing the Demos: Neoliberalism's Stealth Revolution* (New York: Zone Books, 2015).

3. Ibid., 18, 200.

4. For a critical account of that sad compatibility, suggesting that it is, worse still, a cover for pseudo-democratic order that only ever existed as fantasy, see Jodi Dean's review of Brown, "Neoliberalism's Defeat of Democracy," *Critical Inquiry*, October 27, 2015. According to Dean, the shell of democracy that now remains is all it ever was.

5. Brown thinks that such sphereism now "understates" the problem, as she says of Timothy Kuhner's otherwise "analytically astute" analysis of the *Citizens United* decision, which treated corporate campaign contributions as limitless free speech. Kuhner, she says, "terms the decision 'neoliberal jurisprudence' insofar as it applies neoclassical economic theory to the political sphere, analogizes that sphere to the market, and ultimately undoes what he calls the boundary between democracy and capitalism, 'two different systems that belong to two very different spheres.'" Brown argues that we have gone well past cross sphere contamination, however: "Rather, in what Foucault identified as the signature move of neoliberal rationality, the

[*Citizens United*] decision recasts formerly noneconomic spheres *as* markets at the level of principles, norms and subjects" (155).

6. On this point, in particular, see John Schaar's critique of Walzer's compartmentalization in "The Question of Justice," *Raritan* 3, no. 2 (1983). Jacques Rancière, in a forthcoming essay on the concept of "occupation" in *Political Concepts*, proposes that proprieties like that promoted by Walzer are less a standard than a problem for radical democratic politics. Rancière does not discuss Walzer, but he does criticize Arendt, and his critique of Arendt extends equally to Walzer's sphereism. Arguing that in *The Human Condition* Arendt misguidedly binds each activity to its proper location in order to enable politics, Rancière says that the result of such binding looks more like the police than the political—part of the *arche* politics of *rule* that he opposes in favor of freer more tumultuous practices of politics. For Rancière, democratic politics happens precisely in sites of confusion, where it is unclear what is political and what is not, who are the people and who are not. This means that the transformation of the private into a public affair, the great original sin of modernity, which takes the form of the "social" on Arendt's account, is for Rancière the great task of political life. For him, the social, which Arendt sees as the great problem for politics proper, *is* politics. I once made a similar argument, suggesting however that Arendt's own theory provides the grounds for scrambling her strict phenomenological categories; see *Political Theory and the Displacement of Politics* (Ithaca, N.Y.: Cornell University Press, 1993), also "Toward an Agonistic Feminism," in *Feminist Interpretations of Hannah Arendt*, ed. Bonnie Honig (University Park: Pennsylvania State University Press, 1995). Here I continue the effort to engage Arendt's work hoping to find guidance for our particular moment in which the dangers and the promise of the social, which may be occupied by us (Rancière) or which may occupy us (Arendt, Walzer, Brown), are a key issue.

7. "It is hard to think of other places that so fully combine beauty with being public—and that were originally designed for the public," says Joshua Cohen in a lovely rumination on beauty as a democratic experience: "So the experience of something beautiful is an experience of something that draws your attention and then absorbs it," he says. Joshua Cohen, *Gilded Birds* (blog), January 2, 2013: https://gildedbirds.com/2013/01/02/joshua-cohen.

8. Common in relation to a commons is Christopher Breu, *Insistence of the Material: Literature in the Age of Biopolitics* (Minneapolis: University of Minnesota Press, 2014). I discuss differences between the commons and public things in the Epilogue to these lectures.

9. The same is true of property, for example, which can be seen as an insulation from vulnerability, a source of mastery, *or* as a practice that embeds owners into mutuality. See Jill Frank, "Democracy and Distribution: Aristotle

on Just Desert," *Political Theory* 6 (1998): 784–802, and *A Democracy of Distinction: Aristotle and the Work of Politics* (Chicago: University of Chicago Press, 2005).

10. *Calvin and Hobbes,* Bill Watterson. I am grateful to Noah Whinston, who taught me to love *Calvin and Hobbes* and to appreciate its genius.

11. On the threat of and/or desire for dispersion or disintegration in Winnicott, see my reading of *The Bacchae* in "Out Like a Lion," in *Politics, Theory, and Film: Critical Encounters with Lars von Trier,* ed. Bonnie Honig and Lori J. Marso (New York: Oxford University Press, 2016).

12. Brown, *Undoing the Demos,* 200 and passim. Brown's book came out two years after I gave my Thinking Out Loud lectures, so I could not refer to it at the time. I have incorporated some discussion of the book here because her concerns are close to mine and she is one of the few working in democratic theory today to pose these questions in this way. Also, her focus on democratic subjectivity and neoliberal rationality occasions some elaboration of my choice in *Public Things* to pose some of the same questions by way of democratic objects, or object-ivity, and affect. For my own discussion of Rousseau's paradox of politics, with reference to the other discussions of it that preceded my own, see *Emergency Politics: Paradox, Law, Democracy* (Princeton: Princeton University Press, 2009), Chapter 2.

13. On this point, see *Democracy and the Foreigner* (Princeton: Princeton University Press, 2001), Chapter 1.

14. Fortunately, miracle can be an everyday experience; or better, as I argued in *Emergency Politics* with Franz Rosenzweig's help, miracle is a way of experiencing the everyday. But miracles do not come out of nowhere. Or, if they do, we can miss them and then they leave no trace. They require attentiveness, receptivity, preparation, orientation. This is the task of Rosenzweig's great book *The Star of Redemption,* which may be read as a kind of education to miracle. The text itself presupposes and teaches attentiveness, receptivity, preparation, orientation. The Judaic liturgy and calendric cycle, on Rosenzweig's account, also press us in these directions, over and over again. Democratic theorists may learn from Rosenzweig. Receptivity to miracle has its secular political analogues, one example of which is the power of public things to gather us together and the importance of civic ritual and dissent to remind us of their varied importance to us.

15. Brown, *Undoing the Demos,* 200.

16. Ibid., 220.

17. Ibid., 39.

18. See Alex Needham, "Toni Morrison: 'We Used to Be Called Citizens. Now We're Called Taxpayers,'" *The Guardian,* October 5, 2015.

19. On the powers and limitations of the jeremiad as genre, see George Shulman's wonderful book *American Prophecy: Race and Redemption in American Political Culture* (Minneapolis: University of Minnesota Press, 2008).

20. See their recent Irish Food Sovereignty Proclamation: "We recognise that agriculture in Ireland has moved from a polyculture of animals and crops to a monoculture of grass. That for the last forty years farmers have been pushed to produce quantity, not quality. We see how the livelihoods of farming communities have been dismantled . . . ." http://www .foodsovereigntyireland.org/proclamation.html. On seed banking, a practice that is thousands of years old but is threatened by the worldwide spread— exportation—of industrial agriculture since the 1970s, see also the opinion piece by Najma Sadeque, "Control by Seed," *Tribune Express*, February 28, 2012.

21. "Indigenous Mayans Win Stunning Repeal of Hated 'Monsanto Law,'" *Earth We Are One*, November 11, 2015.

22. Here, in a nutshell, is why I am focusing on public things and not on the commons as others may prefer to do. I think there is room for some shared goods to be treated as commons and others as public things, so we do not need to choose one over the other; at least it is not conceptually necessary to do so. I am looking at public things in particular precisely because they postulate sovereignty, still very much an aspiration for those who have been deprived of it, and because public things may (if my Arendtian-Winnicottian reading is right) provide orientation to those who seek further to democratize power among citizens of sovereign states. "The simplest way of contrasting a public and common good is to ask: Does this particular resource require management as a social mandate or is it an expression of social mutuality and collaboration? In other words, is this property best maintained by govern- ment or the public?" says James B. Quilligan: "Why Distinguish Common Goods from Public Goods?" in *The Wealth of the Commons: A World Beyond Market & State*, ed. David Bollier and Silke Helfrich (The Commons Strategy Group, 2012). This question begs the question of whether and how govern- ment can itself be commandeered through social movement politics and other mechanisms to function "as an expression of social mutuality and collaboration."

23. Noortje Marres, "Frontstaging Nonhumans: Publicity as a Constraint on the Political Activity of Things," in *Political Matter: Technoscience, Democ- racy, and Public Life* (Minneapolis: University of Minnesota Press, 2010). Marres concedes that Latour's position is improved when he moves from matters of fact to matters of concern.

24. See James Scott, *Two Cheers for Anarchism: Six Easy Pieces on Autonomy, Dignity, and Meaningful Work and Play* (Princeton: Princeton University Press, 2014), regarding the importance of the infrapolitical register of dissent and alternative forms of life.

25. See John Seabrook, "Sowing for Apocalypse: The Quest for a Global Seed Bank," *The New Yorker*, August 27, 2007.

26. Brown, *Undoing the Demos*, 220, italics original.

27. At the heart of the political invoked by Brown is the polis: a place, a set of buildings (as Arendt points out), squares, streets, sidewalks, market-places, assemblies, and things. Arendt refers more than once to the role of architecture, public and private, in designing a polis for politics. Brown's focus on rationality seems broader—the issue is about how we think now—but this epistemological focus, which yields incredibly powerful and persuasive insights, also pulls us back from the architectural and ontological registers of things. See Patchen Markell, "Arendt's Work: On the Architecture of *The Human Condition*," *College Literature* 38, no. 1 (Winter 2011): 15–44, on how the houses were set in ancient Athens, and Jane Jacobs, *The Death and Life of Great American Cities* (New York: Modern Library, 2011) on how urban design matters for political or collective life. If I close with Hans Monderman in the Epilogue, it is due in part to my sense that design has a key role to play in the staging of democratic possibilities, a point Rousseau understood well.

28. See Ben Hewitt, *The Town That Food Saved: How One Community Found Vitality in Local Food* (Emmaus, Pa.: Rodale Books, 2011).

29. "Unist'ot'en Camp: Holding Their Ground Against Oil & Gas Pipelines," November 18, 2015: https://www.youtube.com/watch?v =5qUw3bqIHks. Notably, given my focus in the next chapters on public things as "holding environments," holding is a key term for the activists.

30. Ibid., emphasis added.

31. On how infrastructure matters, see Bruce Robbins: "unlike commodi-ties, infrastructure is the object of no one's desire, or no one but a few passionate amateurs. It is not artfully illuminated in a shop window for all to see but tucked away out of the usual sight lines, indeed often inaccessible to all but authorized personnel—personnel who (perhaps because funds have dried up) are here conspicuous by their absence. Infrastructure smells, it seems, because attention is not paid, because it is neglected. And it is ne-glected because it belongs to the public domain, all other tokens of belonging effaced, owned in effect by no one. The smell of infrastructure is the smell of the public." It is also an opening to the commons: "Public regulation of utilities that are necessary to life is one of the explicit demands of the recent alter-globalization movement, which has brought a welcome renovation of the concept of the commons." Robbins, "The Smell of Infrastructure: Notes toward an Archive," *boundary 2* 34, no. 1 (2007): 26 and 33. Robbins cites Christopher Otter: "Infrastructure—roads, sewerage, gas mains—is [in-tended to] implant and make durable spaces within which the self-control apposite for civil behavior becomes possible." If so, then infrastructural smell is a sign that the nineteenth-century project of civility has failed, or is in

danger of failing—a sign that we are in danger of falling into barbarity. Christopher Otter, "Making Liberalism Durable: Vision and Civility in the Late Victorian City," *Social History* 27, no. 1 (January 2002): 4. See also Otter, "Cleansing and Clarifying: Technology and Perception in Nineteenth-Century London," *Journal of British Studies* 43, no. 1 (January 2004): 40–64. All this leads Robbins to risk the following important thought: "An analogy presents itself between the practice of the humanities and the humble activities of maintenance" (28).

32. A great deal of the political work of belonging in a democracy involves coming to "matter." The public or the universal always excludes something or someone and the work of belonging involves claiming, reframing, demanding so as to come to matter.

33. The Confederate flag, for example, flown in some state capitols, has for decades re-marked African Americans as unequal by proclaiming fidelity to the pre–Civil War South and the system of juridical slavery. For many Americans, therefore, that flag, flown for decades from the South Carolina statehouse, was never the "public thing" it was claimed to be: It is a divisive thing and an "emblem of hate." Brittney Cooper, "The Confederate Flag Isn't Just a Symbol: Why America's Emblems of Hate Matter—and Their Disappearance Should Be Celebrated," *Salon*, July 1, 2015.

34. Romand Coles, *Beyond Gated Politics: Reflections for the Possibility of Democracy* (Minneapolis: University of Minnesota Press, 2005). Little noted in the stories told of the school integration in Little Rock, Arkansas, is the fact that in September 1958, "one year after Central High was integrated, Governor Faubus closed Little Rock's high schools for the entire year, pending a public vote, to prevent African-American attendance" (http://www .history.com/topics/black-history/central-high-school-integration). In sum, while the diminution of public things in the United States is surely due to over thirty years of neoliberalization, it is connected as well to whites' response to the integration of public things since the civil rights movement.

35. Brittney Cooper, "The Notion of White Safety Has Its Foundations in Indigenous, Black and Brown Unsafety" and "America's War on Black Girls: Why McKinney Police Violence Isn't about One Bad Apple," *Salon*, June 10, 2015.

36. On the unreality of the "real" often enlisted by so-called realists, see my essay with Marc Stears, "The New Realism: From Modus Vivendi to Justice," in *Political Philosophy versus History? Contextualism and Real Politics in Contemporary Political Thought*, ed. Jonathan Floyd and Marc Stears (New York: Cambridge University Press, 2011).

37. For other examples of lived alternatives now, see Jeffrey Stout, *Blessed Are the Organized: Grass Roots Democracy in America* (Princeton: Princeton

University Press, 2010), and my brief discussion of his book in "Three Models of Emergency Politics," *boundary* 2 4, no. 2 (2014).

38. Brown, *Undoing the Demos*, 222. Brown's book does not look into the question of what made the market attractive as a solution to the problems of politics in the first place. When markets decide value, we avoid certain political brawls, such as those over race, civil rights, imperial wars, and poverty that gripped the United States at midcentury. The attraction of the market, as Brown knows, is precisely its promise of a neutral adjudication of value: "In letting markets decide our present and future, neoliberalism wholly abandons the project of individual and collective mastery of existence." (In a footnote, she adds: "While its critique is supremely important, contemporary prescriptive posthumanism expresses the historical conjuncture and colludes with it"; 280 n. 45.) "The neoliberal solution to problems is always more markets, more complete markets, more perfect markets, more financialization, new technologies, new ways to monetize. Anything but collaborative and contestatory human decision making, control over the conditions of existence, planning for the future; anything but deliberate constructions of existence through democratic discussion, law, policy. Anything but the human knowledge, deliberation, judgments, and action classically associated with *homo politicus*" (222).

39. Brown, *Undoing the Demos*, 219.

40. One way of describing my difference with Brown is by juxtaposing Winnicott to Rousseau/Tocqueville. The infrastructure of citizenship whose loss Brown laments was understood by Rousseau and Tocqueville to be itself dependent upon other material conditions: for Rousseau, small republic, territory insulated from outsiders by fortuitous natural circumstances, and so on; for Tocqueville, the shedding of Old World hierarchies in a new world of social equality in a small township structure, and so on. Both thinkers understood that a large territory with a mobile population would undo the infrastructure of citizenship and attenuate the ties on which democratic self-governance, as they understood it, depends. Such localism seems also to animate Brown's vision. Since public things are not just national but also the shared commons of the local, there is nothing about the argument presented here in favor of public things that prejudices the case for large or small democracy.

41. Brown, *Undoing the Demos*, 45, emphasis added.

42. Ibid., 146ff.

43. Ibid., 221–222.

44. Ibid., 21.

45. Ibid., 222.

46. For a similar view, though more critical in more detail of the object oriented ontology approach, see Christopher Peterson, "The *Gravity* of

Melancholia: A Critique of Speculative Realism," in *Politics, Theory and Film: Critical Encounters with Lars von Trier*, ed. Bonnie Honig and Lori J. Marso (New York: Oxford University Press, 2016).

47. Brown, *Undoing the Demos*, 280 n. 45.

48. And it doesn't always start what it is supposed to. On this point and the politics generated by it more generally, see James Martel's fabulous *The Misinterpellated Subject* (Durham, N.C.: Duke University Press, 2017).

49. See, for example, "The Inside Story of the Campaign that Killed Keystone XL," *Vox Energy and Environment*, goo.gl/oDqBi2, which makes clear that a lot of U.S. activists put in a lot of time working on that project, developing tactics, and refining strategy. Their ultimate victory was due to all that, but not only to that. Fortuna smiled on them too: The final stroke leading to their victory, though the article here cited does not say this, was surely the fortuitous election—which they could not have predicted or relied upon—of a new Liberal government in Canada in the fall of 2015.

50. My discussion of this example draws on material that appeared in my post "After Sandy: the Politics of Public Things" on the blog, "The Contemporary Condition," November 5, 2012: goo.gl/l6RcUU.

51. Ben Cohen, "After Sandy, Wired New Yorkers Get Reconnected with Pay Phones," *Wall Street Journal*, October 31, 2012.

52. They are not now publicly owned (they are now serviced by thirteen different local pay phone franchises), but public phones are regulated by New York's Department of Information Technology and Telecommunications.

53. This describes, uncannily, Winnicott's "good enough mother" who secures the holding environment in which the child plays autonomously: Invisible, but when she's needed, she's there.

54. Hannah Arendt, *The Human Condition* (Chicago: University of Chicago Press, 1998), 52.

55. This is the alternative understanding of miracle I explore via Franz Rosenzweig in *Emergency Politics*, in which miracle does not come from above to interrupt the human world but rather emanates from the human world to crystallize something about it.

56. Noting the disinvestment in the United States in public infrastructure and the specially devastating impact on the poor, see Iris Young, "Katrina, Too Much Blame, Not Enough Responsibility," *Dissent* 53, no. 1 (Winter 2006): 41–46.

57. I note, however, that as of March 2016, National Park planners have a plan for expanding the philanthropic options for the system: "The Park Service still won't recognize donors with advertising or marketing slogans. But for the first time, their logos will get prominent display." See the *Washington Post*, May 9, 2016. On the not public but violent history of the system, see

Mark David Spence, *Dispossessing the Wilderness: Indian Removal and the Making of the National Parks* (New York: Oxford University Press, 1999) and Francie Latour, "Hiking while Black: The Untold Story," *Boston Globe*, June 20, 2014.

58. Lear's *Radical Hope: Ethics in the Face of Cultural Devastation* (Cambridge, Mass.: Harvard University Press, 2006) is discussed in detail in Lecture Three, and Hanna Pitkin's "just do it" is the coda of her great book on Hannah Arendt, *The Attack of the Blob: Hannah Arendt's Concept of the Social* (Chicago: University of Chicago Press, 1998).

59. An opt-out is the inverse of a buy-in, which Brown talks about in *Undoing the Demos.* Buy-ins and opt-outs obviously presuppose each other.

60. Alan Blinder and Tamar Lewin, "Clerk in Kentucky Chooses Jail over Deal on Same-Sex Marriage," *New York Times*, September 3, 2015.

61. On Hobby Lobby, see Brown's fine discussion in *Undoing the Demos.*

62. In a way, I suppose this part of my argument comes close to the one pressed by Sandel against Rawls a long time ago.

63. I myself argued in favor of such a choice in "Difference, Dilemmas, and the Politics of Home," in *Democracy and Difference: Contesting the Boundaries of the Political*, ed. Seyla Benhabib (Princeton: Princeton University Press, 1996), claiming that Williams's subject of integrity was too purist, and since we are all always already infiltrated by discourses, values, and goals with which we do not identify, we may risk impurity for political purposes. My aim then was to suggest we are less morally precarious than Williams's argument suggests and resilient enough to risk political impurity. My aim now is not to favor his account of integrity, after all, but to use the schematic present in his argument to organize the issues around buying in and opting out that an argument in favor of public things presses us to consider.

64. Another such mechanism is Ariella Azoulay's recently developed idea of a "right not to be a perpetrator." This right is more than an expression of disavowal. It does not just say "not in my name," which disavows but seems to accept that inevitably things we abhor will be done: the state will do them, but "not in *my* name" please, though in so saying we are also publicly pleading with the state and with others to join us to change the state's behavior. What is interesting about invoking a right not to be a perpetrator is that it acknowledges that there is no opting out. If the state commits acts of violence, I *am* a perpetrator. This is the complaint. Ariella Azoulay, "'We,' Palestinians and Jewish Israelis: The Right Not to Be a Perpetrator," *South Atlantic Quarterly* 114, no. 3 (2015): 687–693.

65. See my discussion in the Preface of my habit of opting out of security lines and the passive-aggressive dance whereby that right to opt out is claimed—a series of speech acts are demanded by the TSA and then consent

to a body search, and so on. The dance has a productive effect. It distracts attention from the real opt-outs.

66. Fredric Jameson, *The Seeds of Time* (New York: Columbia University Press, 1994), xii.

LECTURE TWO. CARE AND CONCERN: ARENDT WITH WINNICOTT

1. The quote is from *Eichmann in Jerusalem*, actually, where the conditions of fitness are not just stability and durability but also plurality: a willingness to share the earth with others. Hannah Arendt, *Eichmann in Jerusalem: A Report on the Banality of Evil* (New York: Penguin Books, 2006).

2. A great example of something like that circularity in relation to public things is provided by Corey Robin with regard to the City University of New York (CUNY) in 2016, where public disinvestment produced administrative disaffection and vice versa. In a blog post, Robin tracks the deterioration of a great public university and lauds the sheer willpower by dint of which many faculty continue to offer high-quality education to students who are often first generation. Noting "how wearying and dispiriting [the] relentless shabbiness can be," Robin says: "While you're striving to inculcate excellence in your students, to get them to focus on the lyrical beauty of a passage in Plato or the epigrammatic power of a line from Machiavelli, you have to literally shut your eyes to the space around you, lest its pervasive message of 'What's the point? Give up' get inside your head. Or the students'." Corey Robin, "The Relentless Shabbiness of CUNY: What Is to Be Done?" May 29, 2016: goo.gl/clEILA.

3. Hannah Arendt, *The Human Condition* (Chicago: University of Chicago Press, 1998), 22.

4. As I noted in Lecture One, citing Ella Myers.

5. Arendt, *The Human Condition*, 55.

6. Ibid., 11.

7. Care and concern receive most attention from Arendt in her essay "The Crisis in Education." When I gave a different version of this lecture at CUNY Graduate Center in March 2016, Jen Gaboury asked me why I don't talk about "care" in Arendt. I said that I was not drawn to the "care" literature and did not want to absorb Arendt into it. Lori Marso suggested that I *was* talking about care, in fact, since this is precisely what the holding environment does, as theorized by Winnicott, and she was right. Earlier that month, at Pomona College, John Seery and some of his students urged me to spend more time on Winnicott's account of "concern." These prods and comments all came together to make me see that not only was I drawn to care and concern in these thinkers in ways I myself had not appreciated, but I was now also ready to say so. This was very helpful to me in the final round of revision,

and I want to thank Corey Robin for inviting me to speak at CUNY and John Seery for hosting me at Pomona.

8. Winnicott does have a short essay on democracy, introduced by Martha Nussbaum: "Some Thoughts on the Meaning of the Word Democracy," in *The Family and Individual Development* (New York: Routledge, 2006). Nussbaum elsewhere argues that Winnicott's views of holding environment and culture could inform a democratic idea of flourishing while underwriting a commitment to a humanistic education. So she thinks there is a politics of some sort here.

9. Winnicott, *The Maturational Processes and the Facilitating Environment: Studies in the Theory of Emotional Development* (New York: Karnac, 2007).

10. Winnicott, quoted in Adam Phillips, *Winnicott* (London: Fontana, 1988), 15, cited in Phyllis Crème, "The Playing Spectator," in *Little Madnesses: Winnicott, Transitional Phenomena, and Cultural Experience*, ed. Annette Kuhn (New York: I. B. Tauris, 2013), 50.

11. Thus, her critique of liberalism and of modern economics is their treatment of property as wealth, which deprives property of its thing-like traits and functions. They promote "the private activities of property-owners and their need of government protection for the sake of accumulation of wealth at the expense of the tangible property itself" (*The Human Condition*, 71–72). She identifies that accumulation with the natural processes of growth that belong to Labor.

12. Arendt, *The Human Condition*, 55.

13. John Kiess is a notable exception. He notes that for Arendt the common world includes "the built environment of cities and towns, monuments and parks, roads and bridges" (99) and talks about infrastructure in Chapters 3 and 4 of his book *Hannah Arendt and Theology* (London: Bloomsbury T&T Clark, 2016).

14. The inclusion of farming or land cultivation in Labor flies in the face of some commentators' claims that Arendt's Labor is the domain of what is historically women's work; see, e.g., Margaret Canovan, *Hannah Arendt: A Reinterpretation of Her Political Thought* (Cambridge: Cambridge University Press, 1994), 124. The point about land cultivation is made at the beginning of the chapter on Work, and so maybe some commentators just missed it. I say more about the gendering of Labor and Work later.

15. The muteness is key, not only to connect labor with animality but also with Winnicottian infancy: "Actually the word infant implies 'not talking,'" Winnicott says in "The Theory of the Parent-Infant Relationship," *International Journal of Psycho-Analysis* 41 (1960): 585–595, at 587.

16. Another seldom noted commonality is that both are characterized as subject to processes. Labor is the domain of natural processes; this is well known. But Action, too, is subject to similar forces: it is a "process" that is set

"into motion," Arendt says (185), noting that its "consequences are boundless" and that in Action "every action becomes a chain reaction" and "every process is the cause of new processes" (190). Without the reifying powers of Things, "the living activities of action, speech, and thought would lose their reality at the end of each process and disappear as though they had never been" (95). The process-like traits of the *vita activa* are normally associated by Arendt's readers with the natural domain of labor, and not with Action. In fact, where Labor and Action seem to differ is in Action's capacity to provide, out of its own inner resources, a stopgap to the process-like consequences of human agency: This is the contribution of promising and forgiveness. Labor is dependent for the analogous provisions exclusively on the outside interventions of Work.

17. Patchen Markell's very fine reading of *The Human Condition* is also focused on Work, though not on Things per se. Instead of Arendt's Labor, Work, Action—the triad from which most commentators begin—Markell suggests that we should be led by the text's overlaps and liminalities to read Arendt's project as "the fraught conjunction of two different pairs of concepts—labor and work, and work and action" (18). Since Work is in *both* pairs, its centrality to Arendt's project is undeniable: Work is "the point at which her two pairs of concepts meet, and at which the structure of the book, like a Mobius strip, twists over on itself." Patchen Markell, "Arendt's Work: On the Architecture of *The Human Condition*," *College Literature* 38, no. 1 (Winter 2011): 15–44.

18. Arendt, *The Human Condition*, 135.

19. Although I emphasize the distinctive traits of the three domains, I note also their points of overlap (as do other commentators on Arendt like Canovan and Markell). One liminal activity between Labor and Work is land cultivation. Does it produce a Thing of lasting enough quality to count as Work? Arendt considers the question at the start of the Work section of *The Human Condition*. Her rumination belongs to a long tradition in political theory that has, for the most part, licensed the occupation of Native lands and the dispossession of Native peoples on behalf of particular forms of private holding and wealth accumulation of which Arendt is quite critical. It is unclear, however, whether Arendt's decision to assign land cultivation to the domain of Labor and not Work extends or resists the legacy of that tradition. For a more detailed treatment of that question, noting the ambiguity of Arendt's lines among Labor, Work, and Action, see my "What Kind of Thing is Land? Hannah Arendt's Object Relations, or: The Jewish Unconscious of Arendt's Most 'Greek' Text," *Political Theory* 44, no. 3 (June 2016): 307–336. I take Arendt's attention to the question of the status of "land" in *The Human Condition* to open the way for Lecture Three's consideration of land as a public thing, in dialogue with Jonathan Lear and Lars von Trier.

20. Arendt, *The Human Condition*, 126.

21. Markell says that Arendt shifts during the course of her treatment of Work. Its objects are first characterized as physically durable (*The Human Condition*, 136–137, cited by Markell, "Arendt's Work," 32), by contrast with Labor and its immediate consumption, but she moves, within the treatment of Work, from durability (of objects) to permanence (via art). Perhaps durability teaches permanence: object permanence is *the experience of objects as stable*, reliable, durable, lasting, and capable of giving to fluctuating subjects some compass-like orientation in a world of flux.

22. As Hanna Pitkin notes, this trait of immersiveness becomes characteristic of the Social, that bastard offspring born of Labor's spread into all other domains of the *vita activa*, which Pitkin compares to the 1950s monstrous film creature, the blob, and which she also identifies with the boundary threatening "bad mother."

23. The language of maturation may suggest otherwise so it is worth noting that in Winnicott no stage is fully left behind, and so these may be experienced, much like Arendt's Labor and Action, not diachronically but synchronically (see Winnicott's *The Maturational Processes*).

24. D. W. Winnicott, *Playing and Reality* (New York: Routledge, 2005).

25. One exception to this would be her essay "The Crisis in Education," where she expresses views about what children need that do seem connected to concern for them; Arendt, *Between Past and Future: Eight Exercises in Political Thought* (New York: Penguin, 2006).

26. Arendt, *The Human Condition*, 168.

27. Noting this point, too, albeit not with reference to Winnicott, are Daniel Klein, " 'Fit to Enter the World': Hannah Arendt on Politics, Economics, and the Welfare State," *American Political Science Review* 108, no. 4 (November 2014): 856–869, and Markell, "Arendt's Work."

28. Kuhn, *Little Madnesses*, 3.

29. Arendt, *The Human Condition*, 138.

30. Winnicott, *Playing and Reality*, 89–90; italics original. Adam Phillips refers to this as Winnicott's Punch and Judy version of the child's secret dialogue with his object (Phillips, *Winnicott*, 131). Through all this, the object relation is transitional, temporary. At some point the object ceases to hold the child in its thrall and enters into a kind of libidinal limbo. What might this mean for public things? It depends on the libido and the limbo.

31. "In health," however, the infant establishes an independent relationship with the transitional object (which may also be the mother—I am here focused on the thingness of the object, but the object can be another person or body part, about which more below) and an in-between space. Winnicott, that is to say, is not interested primarily in subjects (as in Freud) or in objects

(as in Arendt), but in the spaces between them and the relations *between* them. Says Phillips: "Winnicott was consistently preoccupied . . . with the transitional rather than the conclusive in human experience" (143). To be fair, this interest in relations is, in a different way, also true of Arendt, who coins the term, the "in-between" and who is critical of what happens when the wrong sort of object relations become habitual. That said, what Arendt calls the in-between is the domain of Action where men relate to one another directly, on her account, and without the mediation of objects.

32. Arendt, *The Human Condition*, 11.

33. Winnicott, *Playing and Reality*, 119.

34. Ibid., xvi.

35. Ibid., 17.

36. I have drawn here on Barbara Johnson's fine essay "Using People: Kant with Winnicott," in *Persons and Things* (Cambridge, Mass: Harvard University Press, 2008).

37. Arendt, *The Human Condition*, 52. I see in the passage here quoted both derision for the retreat of Parisians into the charming world of tiny things and also an ironic appreciation of the resilience of the human desire to invest in objects, even as they get smaller and smaller, due to the loss of the public and the disappearance of Work into Labor. Compare Arendt here with Deleuze, who comments in his reading of *Suzanne and the Pacific* in "Desert Islands" that she is "typically Parisian" when her first response to shipwreck is to unload things from the ruined boat onto the island. Robinson Crusoe is wanting for similar reasons, Deleuze charges, as he turns in the essay to posit in the place of these two literary efforts a mythic alternative, not named, but clearly referenced: Noah's ark—which carried not things but a future, via reproduction: a boatful of pairs for mating, and his own family. The Ark is not shipwrecked; it lands on a mountaintop rendered island-like by providential flood, so it is like neither of the two types—oceanic and continental— discussed by Deleuze in this essay. It is a third thing, and this may mark, in Arendtian and Deleuzean terms, its capacity to begin anew. Gilles Deleuze, "Desert Islands," in *Desert Islands and Other Texts: 1953–1974* (New York: Semiotext(e), 2004).

38. In *Moby-Dick*, Starbuck prefers the small objects of trade and commerce to the large glorious chase of the whale. Glory has its costs. In Jonathan Lear, *Radical Hope: Ethics in the Face of Cultural Devastation* (Cambridge, Mass.: Harvard University Press, 2006), irrelevance is also a crucial trait. He analogizes the destruction and exhaustion of the native Crow way of life to what happens to game pieces when the game of chess stops being known and played. The pieces go on the shelf, perhaps as art. They may be bric-a-brac or fetish. But they are no longer what they were (48). No one recalls their

function or purpose. The miniature pieces of Plymouth Rock, noted by Tocqueville, are they like the miniatures of the Parisians who lost their empire and embrace their bric-a-brac? Do the small stones broken off the Rock diminish it or contribute to its survival as a founding fantasy? On Lear, see Lecture Three, and on *Moby-Dick*, see my reading in reply to Eric Santner in *The Weight of All Flesh: On the Subject-Matter of Political Economy* (New York: Oxford University Press, 2016): "Charged: Debt, Power, and the Politics of the Flesh in Shakespeare's *Merchant*, Melville's *Moby Dick*, and Eric Santner's *The Weight of All Flesh.*"

39. The same concern comes up elsewhere in Arendt's work, where the problem again is the displacement of politics by an outsized attention and care devoted to things that don't return the favor. In *The Jewish Writings*, Arendt criticizes Jewish pioneers, *chalutzim*, in early twentieth-century Palestine/Israel. She has some admiration for the new type of man that results from their devotion to communal, agricultural work, but, she says, they fell for the lure of the land, mistook land cultivation for actual politics, and thus left politics and world-care to others whose project of ethnonational sovereignty would ultimately undo more progressive alternatives. Whatever we think of this view and its insulation of the so-called pioneers from implication in the land-dispossession policies of the State of Israel, we can hear its echo in *The Human Condition*, where Parisian miniatures, like the crops of the *chalutzim*, cannot occasion or sustain Arendtian care for the world, one of whose chief traits is plurality (violated by both private-sphere withdrawalism and political ethnonationalism, two versions of the same thing, Arendt might say). Hannah Arendt, Jerome Kohn, and Ron H. Feldman, *The Jewish Writings* (New York: Schocken Books, 2007).

40. Iris Young assigns the blame primarily to "consumerism," which in immigration terms is the "pull." But the "push" in my view is the use in the United States of coercive state powers to drive people out of the public realm and to break up the infrastructure of political action, which includes but is not limited to public things: "Consumerism encourages people to focus on the private spheres of their homes; to this extent home is a counterpart of the capitalist marketplace and a detriment to the solidarity of community and assertive public participation." Young, "A Room of One's Own: Old Age, Extended Care, and Privacy," in *On Female Body Experience: Throwing Like a Girl and Other Essays* (New York: Oxford University Press), 156. Thanks to Lori Marso for calling my attention to this essay.

41. I looked for a third way between dissociation and hyperattachment also in *Democracy and the Foreigner* (Princeton: Princeton University Press, 2001) in a reading the *Book of Ruth* in the context of immigration politics. Here it is worth pointing out that the argument for public things does not treat them as a

"site of communitarian unity" as Myers worries (97), because the subject and the community that are formed in relation to the transitional object are both, to borrow Michael Oakeshott's distinction, more collected than collective. Their formation into a "unit," as Winnicott says, does not result in harmonious unity; both may still experience, post-unification, internal conflicts. (After all, as we shall see, ambivalence is a fundamental affect of the self, for Winnicott.) Here, the opposite of unity is not a lack of harmony, but dispersion. Dispersion, not conflict, is what is overcome when the self or community integrates in a Winnicottian way. Hence: collected, not collective.

42. Cristina Beltran offers an Arendtian analysis of these in "Going Public: Hannah Arendt, Immigrant Action, and the Space of Appearance," *Political Theory* 37, no. 5 (October 2009): 595–622.

43. "The Capacity for Concern," 73. We may think here of Bruno Latour's move from matters of fact to matters of concern: "Can we devise another powerful descriptive tool that deals this time with matters of concern and whose import then will no longer be to debunk but to protect and to care . . . ? Is it really possible to transform the critical urge in the ethos of someone who *adds* reality to matters of fact and not *subtract* reality?" Latour lists *likeability* as a specification for constituting *matters of concern*, along with other conditions like: matters of concern should *matter*, have to be *populated*, have to be *durable*. Latour, "Why Has Critique Run Out of Steam? From Matters of Fact to Matters of Concern," *Critical Inquiry* 30, no. 2 (2004): 225–248.

44. Winnicott, "The Development of the Capacity to Feel Concern," in *Maturational Processes*, 75.

45. Ibid.

46. There is an old Jewish joke about a young boy, seemingly intelligent and healthy, who, by the age of four, five, and then six has not begun to speak. The worried family takes him to doctors and specialists who can find nothing wrong with him. One night at dinner, the mother serves soup to the family, the son takes a spoonful, and says, "Ouch! This soup is too hot!" Stunned, the mother turns to him and says: "You can talk?" "Yes, of course," he replies. "Well, then," she asks: "why haven't you said anything until now?" The son replies: "Till now, everything was fine."

47. Winnicott, "The Development of the Capacity to Feel Concern," 76.

48. Ibid., 77.

49. Arendt, *The Human Condition*, 48 n. 39.

50. Thanks to Megean Bourgeois for research assistance on this point. See Adrienne Rich on *The Human Condition*: "To read such a book, by a woman of large spirit and great erudition, can be painful, because it embodies the tragedy of a female mind nourished on male ideologies. . . . The power of male ideology to possess such a female mind, to disconnect it as it were from the

female body which encloses it and which it encloses, is nowhere more striking than in Arendt's lofty and crippled book." *On Lies, Secrets and Silence: Selected Prose 1966–1978* (Toronto: Norton, 1979), 212.

51. Another key claim is that Action is masculine, modeled on boys in the agon. Hanna Pitkin made the case for that view in the mid-1980s but then seems to reconsider in the late '90s. When she glosses the relevant scholarship in *The Attack of the Blob*, she seems to accept the view that Labor and Work are gendered but Action itself is not: "The *animal laborans* is indeed feminine. Explicating the concept of labor, Arendt, unlike any other theorist who employs the term, stresses the sense of that word associated with giving birth" (166), and "Work, in Arendt's account, is . . . symbolically masculine" (167). Pitkin goes on to complicate matters further by noting that there is a further site of the feminine in *The Human Condition*: The "bad mother" who is "engulfing" and is instanced by "the social as Blob." This is arguably the object-mother who does not withdraw at the proper time and place. That we move from her to the good object- and environment-mothers of Labor and Work suggests we may think Arendt's response to the bad object-mother is to put her in her place. Hanna Pitkin, "Justice: On Relating Private and Public," *Political Theory* 9, no. 3 (1981): 327–352; *The Attack of the Blob: Hannah Arendt's Concept of the Social* (Chicago: University of Chicago Press, 1998).

52. Does Arendt invite a connection between Eve/Labor and Adam/Work? Not really. She says that "the curse by which man was expelled from paradise [was not to] punish him with labor and birth; it only made labor harsh and both full of sorrow." Here it is "man" who is punished with sorrowful birth *and* labor; there is no mention of woman at all. And Adam's work is not Work, actually, not in Arendt's sense, since what is mentioned in the biblical verse she cites here, drawing on the Buber/Rosenzweig translation of the Bible, is the care and tilling of the land. And tilling, Arendt will say in the Work section of *The Human Condition*, belongs to Labor, not Work.

53. Arendt, *The Human Condition*, 116.

54. We can still criticize her for this, of course, but it is less easy to do so. It requires more care.

55. Both build on a kind of gratitude for existence, as well, which finds expression in the Actor's or the child's care or concern.

56. John Kiess, *Hannah Arendt and Theology* (London: Bloomsbury, 2016), 100.

57. Ibid., 103; citing *The Human Condition*, 170.

58. Ibid. Kiess does not say this but I suppose it is possible to say that this is no mere "madeleine" but rather Proust's, and therefore a text, not a pastry, whose lastingness is properly attributed to its membership in the category of Work, not Labor. But a more important point is at issue here than assigning things and stuff to their proper categories. It is also important to note that

I would not joke about Kiess's incredible turn to food to underwrite the table were I not an admirer of Kiess's very good book.

59. I discuss Arendt's reading of Heine in detail in "The Laws of the Sabbath (Poetry): Arendt, Heine, and the Politics of Debt," *UC Irvine Law Review* 5 (2015): 463–482.

60. He adds: "Such care also entails knowing which objects to remove from the realm of use altogether"—like art, which Arendt says "transcends both the sheer functionalism of things produced for consumption and the sheer utility of objects produced for use" (101, quoting *The Human Condition*, 173).

61. Such conflicts in perspective on common things are what make the world common, for Arendt.

62. Jane Bennett, *Vibrant Matter: A Political Ecology of Things* (Durham, N.C.: Duke University Press, 2009); Jörg Kreienbrock, *Malicious Objects, Anger Management, and the Question of Modern Literature* (New York: Fordham University Press, 2013).

63. Arendt, *The Human Condition*, 7.

64. Is she providing a certain magic for Action, when she renders invisible the role of things in generating the sorts of selves capable of Action in concert? That is to say, is she, with this claim, securing a kind of holding environment, or undermining the very idea of one? Thanks to James Martel on this point and several others, too.

65. Strikingly, in at least one version of the ancient fable, Care is intimately associated with handling and holding: "As Care (Cura) was crossing a river, she thoughtfully picked up some mud and began to fashion a human being. While she was pondering what she had done, Jupiter came along. . . . Care asked him to give the spirit of life to the human being, and Jupiter readily granted this. Care wanted to name the human after herself, but Jupiter insisted that his name should be given to the human instead. While Care and Jupiter were arguing, Terra arose and said that the human being should be named after her, since she had given her own body. . . . Finally, all three disputants accepted Saturn as judge. . . . Saturn decided that Jupiter, who gave spirit to the human, would take back its soul after death; and since Terra had offered her body to the human, she should receive it back after death. But, said Saturn, '*Since Care first fashioned the human being, let her have and hold it as long as it lives.*' Finally, Jupiter said, 'Let it be called *homo* (*Latin for human being*), since it seems to be made from *humus* (*Latin for earth*).'" Warren T. Reich, "History of the Notion of Care," in *Encyclopedia of Bioethics*, rev. ed., ed. Warren Thomas Reich (New York: Simon & Schuster Macmillan, 1995), 319–331, emphasis added.

66. I use the term "interpellation" loosely, throughout, not in the strict ideological sense connected with Althusser, but connoting a kind of

absorption into something larger than the self that is not exactly reducible to ideology.

67. Winnicott, *Playing and Reality*, 2.

68. Kuhn, *Little Madnesses*, 5, citing Winnicott, "The Location of Cultural Experience," in *Playing and Reality*, 134.

69. For Arendt's account of authority as augmentation, see Chapter 4 of my *Political Theory and the Displacement of Politics* (Ithaca, N.Y.: Cornell University Press, 2013).

70. Winnicott, *The Maturational Processes*, 73.

LECTURE THREE. HOPE AND PLAY: JONATHAN LEAR'S *RADICAL HOPE* AND LARS VON TRIER'S *MELANCHOLIA*

1. For more on the significance of the telescope, see my "Out Like a Lion," in *Politics, Theory, and Film: Critical Encounters with Lars von Trier*, ed. Bonnie Honig and Lori J. Marso (New York: Oxford University Press, 2016), 356–388.

2. Hannah Arendt, *Origins of Totalitarianism* (San Diego: Harcourt Brace Jovanovich, 1994); *Eichmann in Jerusalem: A Report on the Banality of Evil* (New York: Penguin Books, 2006); *The Jewish Writings*, ed. Jerome Kohn and Ron H. Feldman (New York: Schocken Books, 2007).

3. On this point see my *Political Theory and the Displacement of Politics* (Ithaca, N.Y.: Cornell University Press, 1993), which argues, with Nietzsche, that the subject is the effect and not the cause of promising (Chapter 3).

4. "Big Bird in the Presidential Debate: Mitt Romney advocates cutting funding for Sesame Street, PBS," *The Washington Post*, October 4, 2012. Since the original lectures, I noted the politics around PBS and Big Bird in a blog post on The Contemporary Condition, and later also in a short essay for *NoFo*, from which this paragraph and the next are drawn. These were early efforts; the version here is more developed. Also, here, in the context of Lear and von Trier, there is a larger avian theme to which this big bird belongs, as will become clear shortly. "After Sandy: The Politics of Public Things," The Contemporary Condition (blog), November 5, 2012: goo.gl/l6RcUU; "The Politics of Public Things: Neoliberalism and the Routine of Privatization," *NoFo* 10 (2013): 59–76, 63–64.

5. The amount of money involved is relatively small, since most of the budget of PBS is raised through private fundraising (after private donations and licensing fees, only 6 percent comes from government funds). That is, government contributions to PBS amount to only the tiniest sliver of the federal budget. See Kelly Phillips Erb, "Romney Promises to Cut Taxpayer Funding for PBS (But Says He Still Loves Big Bird)," *Forbes*, October 4, 2012.

6. Suzi Parker, "Big Bird Will Haunt Mitt Romney," *Washington Post*, October 4, 2012.

7. It may be worth noting here that social democracy is itself increasingly depicted by conservatives in the United States as an infantile attachment that needs to be given up. People on welfare or reliant on government programs are described by conservative editorialists as sucking at the teat of democracy when they are well past the time for suckling. They use a quasi-Winnicottian language against the welfare state (e.g., when they say citizens need to be weaned from social democracy) and then cast welfare as an infantilizing blankie that seduces citizens into a dependency they need to give up. Moreover, in the United States the "public" thing is often increasingly racialized as well. If Noel Ignatiev once asked how the Irish became white, it is for us also to ask how the public thing became black. In many contexts today, as Brittney Cooper has argued, and as I noted in Lecture One, "public" has come to mean "black." Cooper, "Segregationists Never Went Away: We Just Call Them 'Small-Government Conservatives' Now," *Salon*, May 27, 2015: goo.gl/GJhdkW.

8. Nor are they subjected to the kinds of government surveillance so often aimed at the poor. The point was made recently by Rep. Gwen Moore (D-WI) who sought to turn the tables with her proposed Top 1% Accountability Act, which required "anyone claiming itemized tax deductions of over $150,000 in a given year to submit a clean drug test. 'By drug testing those with itemized deductions over $150,000, this bill will level the playing field for drug testing people who are the recipients of social programs,' a memo on her bill notes." Bryce Covert, "Congresswoman Who Used To Receive Welfare Wants To Drug Test Rich People Who Get Tax Breaks," *Think Progress*: goo.gl/fWr8A7.

9. Charles Blow came closest to discussing the issues in play when he defended the publicness of public television, which pulled him from a rural home with limited opportunities into a world of education and social mobility. Jon Stewart, with his dismissal of the Big Bird storyline as childish, missed its significance. Lauren Berlant is helpful when she says "the object of desire is not a thing (or even a relation) but a *cluster of promises* (*Cruel Optimism*, 16, emphasis added). Berlant is here echoing Winnicott, though Berlant does not engage his work, to my knowledge. (Charles M. Blow, "Don't Mess with Big Bird," *New York Times*, October 5, 2012; Jon Stewart, "Democalypse 2012: Getting Tough with Big Bird," *The Daily Show on Comedy Central*, October 10, 2012; Lauren Berlant, *Cruel Optimism* (Durham, N.C.: Duke University Press, 2011).

10. Emily Dickinson, " 'Hope' Is the Thing with Feathers," in *The Poems of Emily Dickinson*, ed. R. W. Franklin (Cambridge, Mass.: Harvard University Press, 1999), 314.

11. Arendt found a way to respond to the conundrum: "A quotation from Karl Jaspers that struck Arendt 'right in the heart' and which she chose as the epigraph for *The Origins of Totalitarianism* stresses that what matters is not to

give oneself over to the despair of the past or the utopian hope of the future, but 'to remain wholly in the present.'" Jerome Kohn, "Totalitarianism: The Inversion of Politics," 6: https://memory.loc.gov/ammem/arendthtml/essayb5.html.

12. *"It is a hallmark of the messianically wishful,"* Lear writes, that the world "will be magically transformed—into conformity with how one would like it to be—without having to take any realistic steps to bring it about." Jonathan Lear, *Radical Hope: Ethics in the Face of Cultural Devastation* (Cambridge, Mass.: Harvard University Press, 2006), 151.

13. I thank my fall 2012 graduate seminar at Northwestern, and especially Boris Litvin, Tristan Bradshaw, and Noga Rotem, for writing and conversation about Lear that informed my thinking. I am also grateful to my undergraduate seminar at Brown University, "Democracy Among the Ruins," in the fall of 2013, for thinking through Lear and Tocqueville with me.

14. Lear, *Radical Hope*, 3.

15. The question, posed repeatedly at the start of the book, is never answered. Lear spends his time ruling out a series of wrong answers.

16. Lear, *Radical Hope*, 4.

17. Ibid., 4–5.

18. I am not arguing in favor of these alternatives, just highlighting Lear's interpretative choices.

19. D. W. Winnicott, *Playing and Reality* (London; New York: Routledge, 2005).

20. Arendt, "The Jew as Pariah: A Hidden Tradition," in *The Jewish Writings.*

21. In his essay on concern, Winnicott distinguishes guilt and repair and says that guilt is produced by lack of opportunities to do repair. Concern is the practice of (world) repair. D. W. Winnicott, *The Maturational Processes and the Facilitating Environment: Studies in the Theory of Emotional Development* (New York: Karnac, 2007), 77.

22. Lear, *Radical Hope*, 105.

23. Ibid., 108.

24. Recall Winnicott on object permanence as a product of object use: *the object develops its own autonomy and life, and (if it survives) contributes-in to the subject, according to its own properties* (*Playing and Reality*, 89–90; italics added).

25. D. W. Winnicott, *The Child, the Family, and the Outside World* (Reading, Mass.: Perseus, 1987).

26. Arendt, too, thinks most people's moral compass needs the support of a kind of moral or political infrastructure. But she notes that some extraordinary people can maintain their moral bearings without such supports. When she talks about the German soldier who helped Jews in the Second World War, Anton Schmidt, or she notes the Talmudic tale of the thirty-six righ-

teous people by virtue of whom the world goes on existing, she is talking about the unusualness of those people whose moral compass operates unerringly even when the world around them has gone mad.

27. Lear, *Radical Hope*, 154.

28. Ibid., 100.

29. Ibid.

30. That aviary also included the golden eagle. Ibid., 90–91.

31. Ibid., 90.

32. Ibid., 72.

33. Ibid., 79.

34. Similarly, in Tocqueville, there is also a tracking of diminution from heroic to democratic life, also celebrated by Tocqueville, but not without ambivalence. Alexis de Tocqueville, *Democracy in America*, trans. George Lawrence, ed. J. P. Mayer (New York: Perennial Classics, 2001).

35. Alan Finlayson first suggested to me the importance of the fact that in Lear the dream figures the United States as a natural force, not as a political constellation. This may set up the Crow response as one that greets an inevitability. This will recur, the inevitable force of nature metaphorizing political destruction, in von Trier in *Melancholia*, which I discuss later. Of course, disasters of nature are also political disasters in the climate emergency conditions of late capitalism.

36. Arendt, *The Human Condition* (Chicago: University of Chicago Press, 1998), 52.

37. This is the very Tomb that Arendt says marks the end of the glory days of war, in which greatness could be earned on the battlefield and a name made for oneself. The name of the memorial shows that individuality has been displaced by a war fought by unknowns, nobodies, she says. And the public thing that enshrines it, the memorial, will therefore fail to do the proper work of public things, which is to draw members of the community into relation to one another by way of a common object. Arendt, *The Human Condition*, 161.

38. Santner calls transitional objects elegiac tokens in his book *Stranded Objects: Mourning, Memory, and Film in Postwar Germany* (Ithaca, N.Y.: Cornell University Press, 1990), 25.

39. Lear, *Radical Hope*, 51–52.

40. Ibid., 123.

41. Ibid., 56. Pretty Shield also violates old Crow norms when she strikes a grandchild who disobeys, something that Lear, the communitarian, seems to think would never have happened in the old days when, he implies, tribal subjects fit seamlessly into their assigned social roles and such transgression was unheard of (61).

42. Ibid., 149–151.

43. Jason Frank, "Collective Actors, Common Desires," *Political Research Quarterly* (September 2015): 637–641.

44. Ibid., 27–31.

45. James Martel, "Against Thinning and Teleology: Politics and Objects in the Face of Catastrophe in Lear and Von Trier," *Political Research Quarterly* (September 2015): 642–646.

46. This is the challenge of a book like Naomi Klein's *This Changes Everything: Capitalism vs. the Climate* (New York: Simon & Schuster, 2014). See also the discussion by William Connolly of the "advent of the sixth extinction" in his discussion of Klein's book ("Naomi Klein: In the Eye of the Anthropocene," *The Contemporary Condition*, March 15, 2015: goo.gl/oH1xLv), and in his essay "*Melancholia* and Us" in Honig and Marso, *Politics, Theory, and Film*. There are also several other essays on von Trier's *Melancholia* in that volume by Joshua Dienstag, Christopher Peterson, Thomas Elsaesser, and myself (the last a reading of von Trier with *The Bacchae*, another tale of world-endingness).

47. http://www.imdb.com/title/tt1527186/quotes.

48. Claire is a controlled person with a strong sense of order, symbolized by her coffee-tabled Malevich plates, which Justine removes and replaces with Brueghel and Caravaggio.

49. Winnicott, *Playing and Reality*, 120.

50. Lear, *Radical Hope*, 16.

51. Insofar as she is able to innovate a ritual for the end of the world, Justine is like Lear's Plenty Coup.

52. The environment-mother provides a "constructive aim" which makes tolerable "the idea of destruction of the object-mother in loving . . . ." Winnicott, *The Maturational Processes*, 80.

53. Lawrence Weschler, *Everything That Rises: A Book of Convergences* (San Francisco: McSweeney's, 2007), 7.

54. Ibid., 15.

55. Ibid., 22.

56. Ibid.

57. This is supported by Weschler when he says, citing Benjamin, "For without exception the cultural treasures he surveys have an origin, which he cannot contemplate without horror. There is no document of civilization which is not at the same time a document of barbarism. . . . Barbarism taints also the manner in which it is transmitted from one person to another." Hence the need, Benjamin adds, "to brush history against the grain." Weschler, *Everything That Rises*, 41–42.

58. For this observation about hand-holding at the movies, I am indebted to Charles Barbour.

59. Horkheimer and Adorno say that "the housewife finds in the darkness of the movie theater a place of refuge where she can sit for a few hours with nobody watching, just as she used to look out of the windows when there were still homes and rest in the evening. The unemployed in the great cities [i.e. the homeless] find coolness in summer and warmth in winter in these temperature-controlled locations." Theodor Adorno and Max Horkheimer, *Dialectic of Enlightenment: Philosophical Fragments* (Stanford: Stanford University Press, 2002), 139. It seems uncanny: the housewife and the homeless in this passage are mirrored by, respectively, von Trier's Claire and Justine, the latter only newly unemployed, but more profoundly homeless all along.

60. For the term "ugly feelings," see Sianne Ngai, *Ugly Feelings* (Cambridge, Mass.: Harvard University Press, 2007).

61. These two ways of reading *Melancholia*'s world destruction, as belated symptom or futural fantasy, map onto the two ways of experiencing aggression, as described by Winnicott in *The Child, the Family, and the Outside World*. In one, the power of aggression is expressed in the bold child's sometimes antisocial behavior. In the other, it is experienced, sometimes delusionally, as coming from elsewhere to assault the timid child from outside. (As Libby Anker suggested to me, the outside world under capitalism may itself *be* a source of aggression and not just imagined as such.) Both kinds of children experience aggression, an intensification of what begins, Winnicott says in a rather Nietzschean vein, as "muscle pleasure" (233), the sheer pleasure of movement (which is stilled in the colonial destruction of nomadic life forms and rendered jittery in early cinema's silent films; on this last, see Justus Nieland, cited later in this note). Without romancing the child, but permitting an Arendtian embrace of natality, we may say that the aggression of the timid and bold child expresses a joie de vivre that is not simple and is always already attenuated not just by the pressures of conformity to which Arendt and Winnicott, each in their own midcentury ways, paid such close attention, but also by the modern, civilized prohibition (and medication) of certain kinds of (nonpassive) aggression, even though, or perhaps because, such aggression is a fundamentally important part of any repertoire of resilience, part of the agonism that may open a third way between messianism and despair, or force a dialectic of the two. Justus Nieland, "Killing Time: Charlie Chaplin and the Comic Passion of *Monsieur Verdoux*," *Modernist Cultures* 2, no. 2 (2006): 189–208.

62. It is worth noting, then, as Martel does, that in Plenty Coups' dream, the chickadee was not the only bird. "There were also four war eagles. Quoting a historian, Lear (2006, 91) tells us that in his 'later years [Plenty Coups] wore [a golden eagle] feather on his hat to have this helper with him at

all times.' So the chickadee is, in a sense, complementary to, rather than exclusive of, the other more aggressive bird totems of the Crow that are also carried over into the Crow life after their conquest. Lear writes, 'Plenty Coups was able to create a psychological world in which the traditional virtues of the war-eagle and the new virtues of the chickadee could cohabit. Birds who were not of a feather could nevertheless live together in facing the challenges of the new world' (p. 91)." This means that the chickadee is not the final or teleological meaning of the Crow. One day the eagle may return to take its place. And then we will say not that the chickadee was a thinning out of a thick concept but that it held the place for the return of the eagle. This possibility is obscured, Martel argues, by Lear's teleological thinking.

63. See Connolly, *Melancholia* and Us," in Honig and Marso, *Politics, Theory, and Film.*

64. Tocqueville, *Democracy in America*, 115.

65. Lear, *Radical Hope*, 100.

66. Here I am moving a bit away from Martel who, when he argues that teleology must be countered with counter-teleology, is favoring what we might call homeopathic critique, in which the poison is the cure. I am sympathetic to that view, generally. But when we turn to the individual to solve the problem of rampant individuation and formations of individuality that are made to carry heaving burdens of normativity, I find myself thinking the poison is the poison, not the cure. I note, though, that Martel is right to associate Lear with teleology. In the essay "What Is a Crisis of Intelligibility?" Lear assesses new or resurrected public things, like the Sun Dance, in terms of their (non)relation to their "final cause" (155).

67. This may be unsurprising, since the one who secures the holding environment is often unnoticed. That is part of the task.

68. Adriana Cavarero ruminates on the philosophical (mis)directions of skin in her analysis of vulnerability in "Unbalanced Inclinations," a lecture given at Centre de Cultura Contemporània (CCCB), Barcelona, July 2011.

69. Jonathan Lear, "What Is a Crisis of Intelligibility?" in *Appropriating the Past: Philosophical Perspectives on the Practice of Archaeology*, ed. Geoffrey Scarre and Robin Coningham (Cambridge: Cambridge University Press, 2012), 141–155.

70. Ibid., 154.

71. Ibid.

72. D. W. Winnicott, *The Ordinary Devoted Mother and Her Baby: Nine Broadcast Talks* (London: Pamphlet, 1950).

73. The term, its source, and the reason for it have already been noted.

74. Michael Oakeshott, *Notebooks, 1922–86* (Exeter, UK: Imprint Academic, 2014).

EPILOGUE. PUBLIC THINGS, SHARED SPACE, AND THE COMMONS

1. David Mermelstein, "Two Marian Andersons, Both Real," *New York Times*, February 23, 1997.

2. " 'They have taken an action which has been widely criticized in the press,' [Roosevelt] wrote. 'To remain as a member implies approval of that action, and therefore I am resigning.' " Susan Stamberg, "Denied a Stage, She Sang for a Nation," *National Public Radio*, April 9, 2014.

3. Ibid.

4. Thanks to Naomi Honig for this example. See https://www.youtube .com/watch?v=mAONYTMf2pk.

5. Why did she change the wording? To reflect the fact that " 'We cannot live alone,' she said. 'And the thing that made this moment possible for you and for me, has been brought about by many people whom we will never know.' " Stamberg, "Denied a Stage."

6. Winnicott's reading of the story of Humpty Dumpty as a child grown too big for the mother's lap (hence his "great fall") led me to see the Anderson image this way. Winnicott refers to the period of the child's growing independence from the mother in the holding environment as "the 'humpty-dumpty stage' " and notes: "the wall on which Humpty Dumpty is precariously perched [is] the mother who has ceased to offer her lap." Winnicott, *The Maturational Processes and the Facilitating Environment: Studies in the Theory of Emotional Development* (New York: Karnac, 2007), 75.

7. Alan Pyke, "Top Infrastructure Official Explains How America Used Highways to Destroy Black Neighborhoods," *Think Progress*: goo.gl/ZvT8Ty.

8. http://www.publicsphereproject.org/content/commons. For a more Hayekian version of the idea, see: http://www.onthecommons.org/about -commons. Anti-statism is rejected by Harney, one theorist of the undercommons, on good grounds: "if government essentially produces effects of state in various ways, which seems to be what Tim Mitchell and some of the smarter guys around state theory think, then for me, it's not about being against or for the state, it's being about, as Tronti would say, within and against the state, but also with and for the undercommons of the state. So, I just don't line up on the side that there's a state, there's an economy, there's a society, even that there's state and capital in such a clear way. I have a much more, sort of, phenomenological, if I could use that word which I kind of hate, approach to the state. When you get close to it, there's all kinds of shit going on there. Most of it's bad. Most of the effects are bad. But, at the same time, some of the best study, some of the craziest undercommons people have been working in government agencies, local government agencies at the motor vehicle department" (Stefano Harney in Stefano Harney and Fred Moten, "The Undercommons: Fugitive Planning & Black Study," 143).

9. That power is underdetermining, though: as Christopher Breu points out, "In different elaborations of the idea of the commons by Michael Hardt and Jodi Dean, both theorists make a distinction between the common (as Hardt describes it, 'The result of human labor and creativity, such as ideas, language, affects, and so forth') and the commons ('the earth and all the resources associated with it' the [land, forests, the water, the air, minerals, and so forth]). . . . This distinction runs the danger of again divorcing the linguistic, cultural, and affective from the material, object-oriented, and ecological. If we are to make this distinction, then we also need the injunction no common without the commons." Christopher Breu, *Insistence of the Material: Literature in the Age of Biopolitics* (Minneapolis: University of Minnesota Press, 2014), 196.

10. See, for example, https://roarmag.org/essays/undercommoning -collective-university-education; Harney and Moten, "The Undercommons."

11. A similar argument is powerfully made by Davina Cooper, who lists the various publics (not public things) that interact with and contribute to state institutions and practices. Transformative publics, she argues, have four overlapping registers: un/conditional, improper, liberation, and prefigurative (the last being most like the withdrawalist communities I have mentioned here and throughout). See Cooper, "Transformative State Publics," *New Political Science* 38, no. 3 (2016): 315–334.

12. Monderman, who has since passed away, can be seen lecturing on these topics at www.urbannous.org.uk/udlhml.htm. I take Anthony Foxx to share this faith in the power of design to support what he—but not Monderman— would call policy objectives.

13. I introduce Scott here because, as David Owen alerted me as this manuscript was going to press, James Scott admires Monderman, too. Scott, also a ludic thinker, notes in *Two Cheers for Anarchism: Six Easy Pieces on Autonomy, Dignity, and Meaningful Work and Play* (Princeton: Princeton University Press, 2012), the "anarchist tolerance for confusion and improvisation that accompanies social learning, and confidence in spontaneous cooperation and reciprocity" (xii).

14. Tocqueville also found in traffic trouble a welcome scene of spontaneous cooperation, as Jason Frank points out: "Should an obstacle appear on the public highway and . . . traffic be halted . . . neighbors at once form a group to consider the matter; from this improvised assembly an executive authority appears to remedy the common inconvenience before anyone has thought of the possibility of some other authority already in existence before the one they have just formed . . . There is nothing the human will despairs of obtaining through the free use of the combined power of individuals." Jason Frank, "Collective Actors, Common Desires," *Political*

Research Quarterly (September 2015): 637–638, citing Tocqueville, *Democracy in America* (2003), 220.

15. Scott summarizes Monderman's diagnosis and impact as follows: "the more numerous the prescriptions, the more it impelled drivers to seek the maximum advantage within the rules: speeding up between signals, beating the light, avoiding all unprescribed courtesies. Drivers had learned to run the maze of prescriptions to their maximum advantage. Without going overboard about its world-shaking significance, Monderman's innovation does make a palpable contribution to the gross human product. . . . The effect of what was a paradigm shift in traffic management was euphoria. Small towns in the Netherlands put up one sign boasting that they were 'free of traffic signs' . . . and a conference discussing the new philosophy proclaimed 'Unsafe is safe.'" Scott, *Two Cheers for Anarchy*, 83.

16. "I can't think in terms of a management of the common—because it seems like, to me, the first act of management is to imagine that what's informal or what's already going on requires some act to organize it, rather than to join it, rather than to find ways to experiment with this general antagonism" (Harney, in Harney and Moten, "The Undercommons," 130).

17. Jay Barmann, "Video: Tensions Arise over S.F. Soccer Field Between Neighborhood Kids and Recent Transplants," SFist, October 10, 2014: http://sfist.com/2014/10/10/tensions_arise_over_mission_playgro.php. Two years later the lesson had to be relearned: San Francisco Recreation and Park started a pilot program that allowed people to reserve online sections of Dolores Park, for a fee. "Many parks allow you to reserve eating areas or playing fields for organized sports, but, as SFist notes, the areas in question are 'straight up sections of grass.'" Girl Nathan, "Soon Humans Will Rent Patches of Land in a Public San Francisco Park," *Adequate Man*, May 24, 2016: goo.gl/oLwH3t. The city announced its intention to make the program permanent, the story was reported, protests planned, and the city announced it was dropping the program when the pilot period ended in July. Jack Morse, "[Update] You Can Now Reserve Whole Sections of Dolores Park Grass for Yourself, for a Price," SFist, May 23, 2016: http://sfist.com/2016/05/23/rec _parks_pilot_program_allows_you.php.

18. Pyke, "Top Infrastructure Official Explains How America Used Highways to Destroy Black Neighborhoods."

19. "This Is How You Defeat Nestlé," *Food & Water Watch*, May 20, 2016. A similar example, from Maine, is mentioned in Silvia Federici, "Feminism and the Politics of the Commons," *The Commoner*, January 24, 2011.

20. "Stand your ground—because man was not born to run away, because his color won't run, because again and again the settler must incant the disavowal and target the epidermalised trace of his own desire for refuge—is

only the most notorious iteration of this renewed dispersal and deputisation of state violence, aimed into the fugitive, ambling neighbourhoods of the undercommons" ("The Undercommons"). On moving from refusal to concern, see Harney about Moten, Chapter 8, interview: "When I started working with Fred, social life, to me, had a lot to do with friendship, and it had a lot to do with refusal—refusal to do certain kinds of things. And then gradually I got more and more interested in this term, 'preservation,' where I started to think about, 'well, refusal's something that we do because of them, what do we do because of ourselves?' Recently, I've started to think more about elaborations of care and love. So, my social world is getting bigger with our work. But, each piece for me is still another way to come at what we love and what's keeping us from what we love."

Rousseau, Social Contract
Rosenzweig, The Star
Brown, Unbury the Ghost
Tocqueville, Democracy
Myers, Worthy of Flint
Arendt, HC
Winnicott, Playing, Reality, Maternal and Process

Adorno, Theodor, and Max Horkheimer. *Dialectic of Enlightenment: Philosophical Fragments*. Stanford: Stanford University Press, 2002.

Aeschylus. *Libation Bearers*. In *The Oresteia*, translated by Ian Johnston. Arlington, Va.: Richer Resources Publications, 2007.

Arendt, Hannah. *Eichmann in Jerusalem: A Report on the Banality of Evil*. New York: Penguin Books, 2006.

———. *The Human Condition*. Chicago: University of Chicago Press, 1998.

———. *The Jewish Writings*. Edited by Jerome Kohn and Ron H. Feldman. New York: Schocken Books, 2007.

———. *Origins of Totalitarianism*. San Diego: Harcourt Brace Jovanovich, 1994.

Azoulay, Ariella. "'We,' Palestinians and Jewish Israelis: The Right Not to Be a Perpetrator." *South Atlantic Quarterly* 114, no. 3 (2015): 687–693.

Barber, Benjamin R. "The Art of Public Space: Filling the Empty Streets and Turning Pedestrian Piazzas into True Commons." *The Nation*, August 12, 2009.

Beltran, Cristina. "Going Public: Hannah Arendt, Immigrant Action, and the Space of Appearance." *Political Theory* 37, no. 5 (October 2009): 595–622.

Bennett, Jane. *Vibrant Matter: A Political Ecology of Things*. Durham, N.C.: Duke University Press, 2009.

Berlant, Lauren. *Cruel Optimism*. Durham, N.C.: Duke University Press, 2011.

Breu, Christopher. *Insistence of the Material: Literature in the Age of Biopolitics*. Minneapolis: University of Minnesota Press, 2014.

Brown, Wendy. *Undoing the Demos: Neoliberalism's Stealth Revolution*. New York: Zone Books, 2015.

Canovan, Margaret. *Hannah Arendt: A Reinterpretation of Her Political Thought*. Cambridge: Cambridge University Press, 1994.

Cavarero, Adriana. "Unbalanced Inclinations." Lecture given at the Centre de Cultura Contemporània (CCCB), Barcelona, July 2011.

Cohen, Joshua. Gilded Birds (blog). https://gildedbirds.com.

Coles, Romand. *Beyond Gated Politics: Reflections for the Possibility of Democracy.* Minneapolis: University of Minnesota Press, 2005.

Connolly, William. *The Fragility of Things: Self-organizing Processes, Neoliberal Fantasies, and Democratic Activism.* Durham, N.C.: Duke University Press, 2013.

———. "*Melancholia* and Us." In Honig and Marso, *Politics, Theory, and Film,* 413–421.

———. "Naomi Klein: In the Eye of the Anthropocene." The Contemporary Condition (blog). March 15, 2015. goo.gl/xuJfoq.

Cooper, Brittney. "America's War on Black Girls: Why McKinney Police Violence Isn't about One Bad Apple." *Salon,* June 10, 2015. goo.gl/6ohmTu.

———. "The Confederate Flag Isn't Just a Symbol: Why America's Emblems of Hate Matter—and Their Disappearance Should Be Celebrated." *Salon,* July 1, 2015. goo.gl/WCFgtK.

———. "Segregationists Never Went Away: We Just Call Them 'Small-Government Conservatives' Now." *Salon,* May 27, 2015. goo.gl/e9Ek6A.

Cooper, Davina. "Transformative State Publics." *New Political Science* 38, no. 3 (2016): 315–334.

Coulthard, Glen. *Red Skin, White Masks: Rejecting the Colonial Politics of Recognition.* Minneapolis: University of Minnesota Press, 2014.

Crème, Phyllis. "The Playing Spectator." In *Little Madnesses: Winnicott, Transitional Phenomena, and Cultural Experience,* edited by Annette Kuhn, 39–52. New York: I. B. Tauris, 2013.

Dean, Jodi. "Neoliberalism's Defeat of Democracy." *Critical Inquiry,* October 27, 2015. goo.gl/4orQBR.

Deleuze, Gilles. "Desert Islands." In *Desert Islands and Other Texts: 1953–1974,* 9–14. New York: Semiotext(e), 2004.

Dickinson, Emily. "'Hope' Is the Thing with Feathers." In *The Poems of Emily Dickinson,* edited by R. W. Franklin, 314. Cambridge, Mass.: Harvard University Press, 1999.

Federici, Silvia. "Feminism and the Politics of the Commons." *The Commoner,* January 24, 2011.

Frank, Jason. "Collective Actors, Common Desires." *Political Research Quarterly* (September 2015): 637–641.

Frank, Jill. "Democracy and Distribution: Aristotle on Just Desert." *Political Theory* 26, no. 6 (1998): 784–802.

———. *A Democracy of Distinction: Aristotle and the Work of Politics.* Chicago: University of Chicago Press, 2005.

Harney, Stefano, and Fred Moten. "The Undercommons: Fugitive Planning & Black Study." goo.gl/8Pjzbo.

Hewitt, Ben. *The Town That Food Saved: How One Community Found Vitality in Local Food*. Emmaus, Pa.: Rodale Books, 2011.

Honig, Bonnie. "After Sandy: The Politics of Public Things." The Contemporary Condition (blog), November 5, 2012. goo.gl/wqWBsk.

———. *Antigone, Interrupted*. Cambridge: Cambridge University Press, 2013.

———. "Charged: Debt, Power, and the Politics of the Flesh in Shakespeare's *Merchant*, Melville's *Moby Dick*, and Eric Santner's *The Weight of All Flesh*." In *The Weight of All Flesh: On the Subject-Matter of Political Economy*, 131–182. New York: Oxford University Press, 2016.

———. *Democracy and the Foreigner*. Princeton: Princeton University Press, 2001.

———. "Difference, Dilemmas, and the Politics of Home." In *Democracy and Difference: Contesting the Boundaries of the Political*, edited by Seyla Benhabib, 257–277. Princeton: Princeton University Press, 1996.

———. *Emergency Politics: Paradox, Law, Democracy*. Princeton: Princeton University Press, 2009.

———. "The Laws of the Sabbath (Poetry): Arendt, Heine, and the Politics of Debt." *UC Irvine Law Review* 5 (2015): 463–482.

———. "Public Things: Jonathan Lear's *Radical Hope*, Lars von Trier's *Melancholia*, and the Democratic Need." *Political Research Quarterly*, September 2015.

———. "Out Like a Lion." In Honig and Marso, *Politics, Theory, and Film*, 356–388. New York: Oxford University Press, 2016.

———. *Political Theory and the Displacement of Politics*. Ithaca, N.Y.: Cornell University Press, 1993.

———. "The Politics of Public Things: Neoliberalism and the Routine of Privatization." *NoFo* 10 (2013): 59–76.

———. "Three Models of Emergency Politics." *boundary 2* 4, no. 2 (2014): 45–70.

———. "Toward an Agonistic Feminism." In *Feminist Interpretations of Hannah Arendt*, edited by Bonnie Honig, 135–166. University Park: Pennsylvania State University Press, 1995.

———. "What Kind of Thing Is Land? Hannah Arendt's Object Relations, or: The Jewish Unconscious of Arendt's Most 'Greek' Text." *Political Theory* 44, no. 3 (June 2016): 307–336.

Honig, Bonnie, and Lori J. Marso, eds. *Politics, Theory, and Film: Critical Encounters with Lars von Trier*. New York: Oxford University Press, 2016.

Honig, Bonnie, and Marc Stears. "The New Realism: From Modus Vivendi to Justice." In *Political Philosophy versus History? Contextualism and Real*

Politics in Contemporary Political Thought, edited by Jonathan Floyd and Marc Stears, 177–205. New York: Cambridge University Press, 2011.

Jacobs, Jane. *The Death and Life of Great American Cities*. New York: Modern Library, 2011.

Jameson, Fredric. *The Seeds of Time*. New York: Columbia University Press, 1994.

Johansen, Bruce Elliott, ed. "Trail of Tears." In *The Encyclopedia of Native American Legal Tradition*. Westport, Conn.: Greenwood Press, 1998.

Johnson, Barbara. "Using People: Kant with Winnicott." In *Persons and Things*, 94–108. Cambridge, Mass.: Harvard University Press, 2008.

Kiess, John. *Hannah Arendt and Theology*. London: Bloomsbury T&T Clark, 2016.

Klein, Daniel. "'Fit to Enter the World': Hannah Arendt on Politics, Economics, and the Welfare State." *The American Political Science Review* 108, no. 4 (November 2014): 856–869.

Klein, Naomi. *This Changes Everything: Capitalism vs. the Climate*. New York: Simon & Schuster, 2014.

Kohn, Jerome. "Totalitarianism: The Inversion of Politics." https://memory .loc.gov/ammem/arendthtml/essayb5.html.

Kreienbrock, Jörg. *Malicious Objects, Anger Management, and the Question of Modern Literature*. New York: Fordham University Press, 2013.

Latour, Bruno. "From Realpolitik to Dingpolitik, or How to Make Things Public." In *Making Things Public: Atmospheres of Democracy*, edited by Bruno Latour and Peter Weibel, 14–44. Cambridge, Mass.: MIT Press, 2005.

———. "Why Has Critique Run Out of Steam? From Matters of Fact to Matters of Concern." *Critical Inquiry* 30, no. 2 (2004): 225–248.

Lear, Jonathan. *Radical Hope: Ethics in the Face of Cultural Devastation*. Cambridge, Mass.: Harvard University Press, 2006.

———. "What Is a Crisis of Intelligibility?" In *Appropriating the Past: Philosophical Perspectives on the Practice of Archaeology*, edited by Geoffrey Scarre and Robin Coningham, 141–155. Cambridge: Cambridge University Press, 2012.

Markell, Patchen. "Arendt's Work: On the Architecture of *The Human Condition*." *College Literature* 38, no. 1 (Winter 2011): 15–44.

Marres, Noortje. "Frontstaging Nonhumans: Publicity as a Constraint on the Political Activity of Things." In *Political Matter: Technoscience, Democracy, and Public Life*. Minneapolis: University of Minnesota Press, 2010: 177–210.

Martel, James. "Against Thinning and Teleology: Politics and Objects in the Face of Catastrophe in Lear and Von Trier." *Political Research Quarterly* (September 2015): 642–646.

———. *The Misinterpellated Subject*. Durham, N.C.: Duke University Press, 2017.

Minton, Anna. *What Kind of World Are We Building? The Privatisation of Public Space.* London: Royal Institute of Chartered Surveyors, 2006.

Myers, Ella. *Worldly Ethics: Democratic Politics and Care for the World.* Durham, N.C.: Duke University Press, 2013.

Ngai, Sianne. *Ugly Feelings.* Cambridge, Mass.: Harvard University Press, 2007.

Nieland, Justus. "Killing Time: Charlie Chaplin and the Comic Passion of *Monsieur Verdoux.*" *Modernist Cultures* 2, no. 2 (2006): 189–208.

Nussbaum, Martha. "Dr. True Self. Review of *Winnicott: Life and Work* by F. Robert Rodman." *The New Republic*, October 27, 2003.

Oakeshott, Michael. *Michael Oakeshott: Notebooks, 1922–86.* Exeter, UK: Imprint Academic, 2014.

Obomsawin, Alanis. *Kanehsatake: 270 Years of Resistance.* 1993. Film. https://www.youtube.com/watch?v=7yP3srFvhKs.

Otter, Christopher. "Cleansing and Clarifying: Technology and Perception in Nineteenth-Century London." *Journal of British Studies* 43, no. 1 (January 2004): 40–64.

———. "Making Liberalism Durable: Vision and Civility in the Late Victorian City." *Social History* 27, no. 1 (January 2002): 1–15.

Peterson, Christopher. "The *Gravity* of *Melancholia*: A Critique of Speculative Realism." In Honig and Marso, *Politics, Theory and Film*, 389–412.

Phillips, Adam. *Winnicott.* London: Fontana, 1988.

Pitkin, Hanna. *The Attack of the Blob: Hannah Arendt's Concept of the Social.* Chicago: University of Chicago Press, 1998.

———. "Justice: On Relating Private and Public." *Political Theory* 9, no. 3 (1981): 327–352.

Quilligan, James B. "Why Distinguish Common Goods from Public Goods?" In *The Wealth of the Commons: A World Beyond Market & State*, edited by David Bollier and Silke Helfrich. n.p.: The Commons Strategy Group, 2012.

Rancière, Jacques. "Occupation." *Political Concepts*, forthcoming.

Reich, Warren T. "History of the Notion of Care." In *Encyclopedia of Bioethics*, revised edition, edited by Warren T. Reich, 319–331. New York: Simon & Schuster Macmillan, 1995.

Rich, Adrienne. *On Lies, Secrets and Silence: Selected Prose 1966–1978.* Toronto: Norton, 1979.

Robbins, Bruce. "The Smell of Infrastructure: Notes toward an Archive." *boundary 2* 34, no. 1 (2007): 25–33.

Robin, Corey. "The Relentless Shabbiness of CUNY: What Is to Be Done?" Blog post, May 29, 2016. goo.gl/KnYJSO.

Santner, Eric. *Stranded Objects: Mourning, Memory, and Film in Postwar Germany.* Ithaca, N.Y.: Cornell University Press, 1990.

Scarry, Elaine. *Thinking in an Emergency.* New York: Norton, 2011.

Schaar, John. "The Question of Justice." *Raritan* 3, no. 2 (1983).

Scott, James. *Two Cheers for Anarchism: Six Easy Pieces on Autonomy, Dignity, and Meaningful Work and Play.* Princeton: Princeton University Press, 2014.

Seabrook, John. "Sowing for Apocalypse: The Quest for a Global Seed Bank." *The New Yorker,* August 27, 2007.

Shulman, George. *American Prophecy: Race and Redemption in American Political Culture.* Minneapolis: University of Minnesota Press, 2008.

Simpson, Audra. *Mohawk Interruptus: Political Life across the Borders of Settler States.* Durham, N.C.: Duke University Press, 2014.

Spence, Mark David. *Dispossessing the Wilderness: Indian Removal and the Making of the National Parks.* New York: Oxford University Press, 1999.

Stewart, Jon. "Democalypse 2012: Getting Tough with Big Bird." *The Daily Show on Comedy Central,* October 10, 2012.

Stout, Jeffrey. *Blessed Are the Organized: Grass Roots Democracy in America.* Princeton: Princeton University Press, 2010.

Tocqueville, Alexis de. *Democracy in America.* Translated by George Lawrence, edited by J. P. Mayer. New York: Perennial Classics, 2001.

Weschler, Lawrence. *Everything That Rises: A Book of Convergences.* San Francisco: McSweeney's, 2007.

Winnicott, D. W. *The Child, the Family, and the Outside World.* Reading, Mass.: Perseus, 1987.

———. *The Maturational Processes and the Facilitating Environment: Studies in the Theory of Emotional Development.* New York: Karnac, 2007.

———. *The Ordinary Devoted Mother and Her Baby: Nine Broadcast Talks.* London: Pamphlet, 1950.

———. *Playing and Reality.* New York: Routledge, 2005.

———. "Some Thoughts on the Meaning of the Word Democracy." In *The Family and Individual Development,* introduced by Martha Nussbaum, 228–250. New York: Routledge, 2006.

———. "The Theory of the Parent-Infant Relationship." *International Journal of Psycho-Analysis* 41 (1960): 585–595.

Wittgenstein, Ludwig. *Philosophical Investigations.* Translated by G. E. M. Anscombe. Oxford: Blackwell, 1953.

Young, Iris Marion. "Katrina, Too Much Blame, Not Enough Responsibility." *Dissent* 53, no. 1 (Winter 2006): 41–46.

———. "A Room of One's Own: Old Age, Extended Care, and Privacy." In *On Female Body Experience: Throwing Like a Girl and Other Essays,* 155–170. New York: Oxford University Press.

Monsanto: in Guatemala, 20, 29; in
Iraq, 20
MOOCs (massive open online courses),
19
moods, transitional objects, 44
Moten, Fred, 97
mother-care, 49, 101n4
mourning, 102n10

NAACP (National Association for the
Advancement of Colored People), and
Marian Anderson, 87
natality, 39, 43; destruction and, 80
nationalists, 3
native peoples: Chevron and, 23;
sovereignty and public things, 23
neoliberalism, 13–14; and alternative
political movements, 20; *Citizens
United*, 104n5; citizenship and, 14;
destructiveness and, 56; opting out,
32–34; privatization and, 55–56; racial
politics and, 25; reality testing and, 56;
Walzer on, 14
noncompliance of things, 53–54

Oakeshott, Michael, 16
object destruction, 44–46; reality testing
and, 55–56
object permanence, 2, 39
object relations, 17, 28, 38, 43;
circularity, 46; contribution of object,
45; destructiveness and, 44–46; *The
Human Condition*, 40–41; mother and,
101n4; *versus* object use, 44–45; and
transition objects, 43
object use *versus* object relations, 44–45
objectivation *versus* subjectivation, 15
object-mother, 49; Labor and, 49–50
object-relations theory, 2, 30–31, 40–41
objects, recalcitrance, 59
Occupy movement, 20, 21; limits, 26
Olmsted, Frederick Law, 15–16
opting out: Kentucky clerk and, 32–34;
neoliberalism and, 32–34; suicide
as, 73

Pacific Trail Pipeline, 22–23
park space rental, 96–97
parvenu life, Plenty Coups and, 64
PBS (Public Broadcasting System),
60–61, 123n9
permanence, 45–46, 116n21; *homo faber*
and, 42
Pitkin, Hanna, 32
place attachment, 102n12
Plenty Coups, 10, 32; care for the world
and, 66; Chickadee and, 67–68;
dreaming, 66–67, 69; *parvenu* life,
64; public things, importance,
68–69; radical hope of, 66; social
conformism, 64
polis, 108n27
the political, decline, 14–15
political movements. *See also* alternative
political movements
political spheres: Action, 14–15; Labor,
14; Work, 14
political theory: Action and, 54;
collectivity, 17
political thingness, loss of, 30–31
political things, 3
posthumanism, Brown on, 29
private space: private things in, 48;
repossession, 21
privatization, 3, 97; neoliberalism and,
55–56, 101n6; place attachment and,
102n12; racial politics and, 25
proceduralism, 14
progressive politics, public things
and, 92
property, 105n9
psychoanalysis, 39–40
public phones, 29–30, 31
public realm, closure, 48
public ritual, 62; food and ritual, 69–70
public speech, Action and, 54
public things, 3; Big Bird as figure,
60–61, 123n9; collaborative tending,
92–93; commons-oriented approach,
91–92; definition, 4; democracy and,
4, 90–91; holding environments and

THINKING OUT LOUD: THE SYDNEY LECTURES IN
PHILOSOPHY AND SOCIETY

Dimitris Vardoulakis, series editor

Stathis Gourgouris, *Lessons in Secular Criticism*
Bonnie Honig, *Public Things: Democracy in Disrepair*

classics cave
   Aristotle, Ethics
           Politics

Machiavelli, Prince

Hobbes, Leviathan

Spinoza, Ethics
           Tractatus

Rousseau - assorted

Tocqueville, Democracy